THE COSTUME
COLLECTOR'S
COMPANION
1890-1990

First published 1998 by Aurum Press Ltd.,
25 Bedford Avenue, London WC1B 3AT

Art Direction and Design: Sarah Davies
Illustrations: Pat Fogerty
Photography: Graham Rae
Cartoons: Angela Martin
Photographic Styling: Sue Russell
Costume Assistant: Phoebe Hawthorne
Project Editor: Judy Spours

A catalogue record for this book is available
from the British Library.

ISBN 1 85410 552 3

Printed and bound in Great Britain
by Butler & Tanner Ltd
Frome and London

THE COSTUME
COLLECTOR'S
COMPANION
1890-1990

Rosemary Hawthorne

Illustrated by Pat Fogerty

AURUM PRESS

'Tell me where is fancy bred
Or in the heart or in the head?
How begot, how nourished?
Reply, reply.'

Merchant of Venice
William Shakespeare

CONTENTS

INTRODUCTION

You don't have to be mad to collect costume, but it helps. I have been deranged for nearly thirty years now, and this book is my opportunity to examine the symptoms of this strange disease. After reading it, you may yourself be infected to a greater or milder degree – or you may be completely cured.

Old clothes – also known as period dress, vintage fashion, collectable costume, antique textiles and that old tat – are my thoroughly enjoyable hobby and entertainment. They are also a part of the bread and butter of social history. There is perhaps no better way to see how our lives have progressed than a quick flip through the wardrobes of the past.

Although I also collect clothes from the eighteenth and early nineteenth centuries, I concentrate here on the last hundred years of fashion's history, from the 1890s to the 1990s. This period is a neat, containable time, during which styles of dress changed rapidly, in contrast to earlier centruies when fashion eased its way slowly through changes of style and down the social ladder. I use examples from my own storehouse, a third-floor back bedroom known as the Costume Room. Most are women's clothes, but I toss in the odd man from time to time, usually dressed only in his underpants.

For each decade of the hundred year period, I discuss and illustrate a comprehensive range of the clothes that you are likely to find and will need to recognize, and which are representative styles of the time. I advise you about whether a garment or accessory is rare, fairly unusual or dead common, and I give you a guide as to the price you might expect to pay for it. It is only a guide, as nothing varies more in price than old costume: trash to one is treasure to another. It is a mistake to attempt to collect just for profit. I give you ideas for forming an interesting collection and, in the more recent decades, suggest how you might predict what costume will still be valuable and interesting in the future.

Collections are as individual as the people who build them, and costume fanatics collect for different reasons. You may wish to wear your pieces, whilst I have never had the slightest desire to do so. My collection exists as a piece of social history to illustrate talks, writing and television features. Occasionally, I put my clothes onto dress-makers' dummies, for exhibitions or around the house: our guests at the vicarage get used to meeting apparitions on the stairs.

I have always been interested in clothes and fashion (my mother worked in a London fashion house during most of my childhood), but I didn't start to collect costume until the late 1960s, when I was stuck at home in the country bringing up (almost swamped by) seven children. I am married to a vicar, and as a mother with hardly any spare cash (when has that ever stopped an ardent collector?) I stumbled on antique clothes as a means to satisfy a yearning to possess and handle charming, intriguing artefacts from another age. I started the collection with humble nineteenth-century cotton underclothes that often required a bit of repair, bought from a market dealer. I spent precious free time looking at old clothes in museums, talking to other collectors (who were thrilled to talk about their own passion) and absorbing all possible books and magazine articles about costume history. As a collector, you need to be both an eager student and someone who enjoys the thrill of the chase.

For some people, the idea of old clothes is shudder-making, the assumption being that they are distastefully unclean and will lead to plague or pox. This is stuff and nonsense. You don't have to raid a refuse tip to acquire them (although many fine period clothes find their way here), and my hope is that this book will put the earnestly interested in touch with the unassailably not to their mutual satisfaction. However, be sensitively aware that when people give you clothes they are parting with memories, both happy and sad.

Pass!

Within the pages of this book you will meet my husband, the vicar (who hates collections of anything, which only goes to prove that opposites do attract), my youngest daughter and severest critic, the Arbiter of Good Taste, and Ollie the collie, a dog for whom the word costume has special meaning. And you will meet many and compelling imaginary characters, the women who wore all these marvellous outfits in times past.

THE 1890S REVOLTING DAUGHTERS

If I had to choose one decade from the nineteenth century in which to be a young woman, it would be the 1890s. I would prefer to be part of a family that was if not staggeringly rich, at least comfortably off, where the daughters were well educated – and well dressed. It was a decade of changing attitudes of the young towards their parents. Girls sought more social freedom: they travelled, they studied at universities and they took up careers, an idea which twenty years earlier would have been thought 'poppycock' by their fathers and brothers. They were cultured in the arts, yet played more and more vigorous sports. From the 1880s, the bicycle was popular throughout the social classes, and this craze for cycling probably helped hasten women into trousers, which were styled either as a ladylike divided skirt or, more daringly, as knickerbockers.

This is a splendid era for costume collecting, although it is rare to find original top clothes that haven't been altered. Many were re-vamped to be worn during the next fifty years; two World Wars often had people looking out the 'old stuff' and putting their scissors to work.

For the best, fashionable look of the time we must think of the deliciously dressed Miss Gwendoline

Fairfax of Oscar Wilde's play *The Importance of Being Earnest*. She is presented as a shining example of dressmakers' art in the 1890s, confidently well corseted, leg-of-mutton sleeved, high hatted and swish-trained.

The other important dress trend of the time was influenced by the Aesthetic Movement. Lady poets and like-minded spirits adopted vaguely medieval-inspired clothes (the Pre-Raphaelite artists were always painting pictures of such women) that flowed across the body, the very antithesis of a 'Gwendoline' look. The strangeness of the colours of these garments caused Gilbert and Sullivan to lampoon the whole cult in their operetta *Patience*, in the famous couplet, 'Greenery Yallery, Grosvenor Gallery'. Liberty & Co., London, was the shop to go to for this kind of gear, as it specialized in weird and wonderful textiles, many of them imported from the Orient, and had its own workrooms which could run you up a little number in the latest 'antique' mode. Original 'Aesthetic' dress is hard to discover now: misunderstood after its day, it was often consigned to dressing-up boxes for family charades and hasn't survived to utter one more word of Swinburne.

1890s top and outer clothes were always beautifully tailored. The sewing-machine (first patented in 1851 by Isaac Merrit Singer) now did a firm lock-stitch, enabling fine clothes to be made faster. Superior wardrobes were 'bespoke' (tailored for the individual, requiring lots of hand finishing) and the garments display a wealth of new tailoring techniques, especially those from Paris, which had been the centre of *haute couture* for centuries. But there were also good quality ready-to-wear clothes available, and the ladies' magazines of the 1890s are filled with pages of advertisements for manufactured garments. The fabrics were ravishing – from lustrous silks, brocaded satins and velvets to the more hardy breeds of linen, cotton and woollen cloth. There were also many 'mixed' fibres, twills and worsteds. Generally, although they may not look it, women's clothes were slowly becoming simpler and more practical, emphasizing a small, hand-span waist, curved 'cello' hips and a high, rounded bosom.

The cut of clothes, particularly the two-piece or 'costume', favoured a rather dashing masculinity, with the skirts at walking length for daytime. The blouse and skirt ensemble was popular, with the blouse usually high necked and either severely plain or exquisitely fussy.

Evening dresses plunged at the cleavage and

developed a frou-frou train at the back. Underclothes were sweet, hand-made confections for the wealthy: lavish, embroidered lingerie made of silk or lawn and plenty of it, sets and sets of chemises, drawers, camisoles and petticoats. It was plainer underneath for the less grand – cotton, linen or flannel with a few tucks and a bit of machine-made insertion lace. Those brave spirits seeking women's rights and the full franchise likely wore hygienic combinations, serge knickers and a pair of 'rational' (unboned) stays. Stockings were made from cotton, silk or wool, black being worn for almost every occasion except full evening dress. Shoes and boots had small Louis heels (thick, with a curved-in waist) to offset the fullness at the back of the skirts. Hats were brimmed, but not vast, with shallow crowns, and were usually much decorated with feathers (the Victorians loved dead birds), ribbons or false flowers, and tiny bonnets were still worn, especially by older women.

Women carried charming needleworked fabric purses or small, manufactured leather handbags on metal frames; when biking these were slung from a shoulder strap. Belts were extremely attractive and, to set off the delight of a tiny waist, were often made from shaped metal or had large, eye-catching clasps. And a lady drew on gloves for every conceivable occasion, day and night: she was incorrectly dressed if her hands were not covered in public.

CLOTHES OF THE 1890s

After a bit of delving and umming and aahing about what would be best to show you, I've made a careful selection which characterizes the general look and feel of the period and will give an idea about the sort of clothes you will want to look for. They all present strong images which will help to get your eye in, as antique dealers say. Many of the

> I give many of the dresses in my collection names: sometimes it's the name of their original owner, or, if I don't know that, a name that sums up the personality of the outfit. It's batty, but surely better than calling something 'the red dress' or the 'blue coat'? We might as well start with a bit of upper crust, so, for my first entry here, may I introduce The Honourable Gwendoline Fairfax?

clothes left to us from the nineteenth century belonged to rich people, simply because they had money to purchase them, room to store them and servants to look after them. These were the garments that were conserved, whereas working-class clothes are almost non-existent. The 1890s was technically ten years of superb making. Not only was the sewing-machine first rate, but hand sewing was of a high order and the finish on garments is almost always strong and very neat.

TWO-PIECE COSTUME, machine and hand sewn, in heliotrope (damson jam colour) silk velvet, lined with 'shot' taffeta of the same hue. The fitted bodice, with tiny, flared-back peplum, has full-headed leg-of-mutton sleeves, ending with narrow pointed cuffs and a small, stand collar with lace 'fall'. Inside the bodice are 12 hand-cased (separately hand sewn) whalebones, feather-stitched into place, and it fastens down the front with a row of hooks and eyes. The skirt, which is cut in panels with most of the fullness to the back, is 18 feet around the hem, falling from a 23-inch waist. Hooks fasten the back and there are two large pockets set into the side seams. It was made by a court dress-maker (thus called because she would have understood the rules and niceties involved in making presentation dresses) and her name and address – Madame Fusedale, 87 Wigmore Street, Cavendish Square – are embossed in gold lettering on the waistband and 'stay strap' (a petersham belt within the bodice waist that ensures the top a snug fit). This is a lovely example of High Victorian style, in excellent condition. Miss Fairfax is one of the noblest creatures in my entire collection. About 1895. **£400-500/\$660-825.** (See Plate 2.)

These shop-lifters' pockets are a feature of many dresses, including wedding dresses, of the second half of the nineteenth century.

ASPLENDID PAIR of ladies' knickerbockers made from tough cotton in a grey-blue colour. Breeches shape, caught at the knee with a buttoned band, I am certain these went on many a bicycle ride in the 1890s. At the back there is a flap of material, secured by three large white buttons, that can at a moment's notice 'let down' to facilitate a need. But the charm of this pair of knickerbockers lies in the red and white label sewn on the outside of the flap, which reads 'MILLENNIUM Made from HOYLE'S SAMSON DRILL. IMITATORS BEWARE'. About 1895. **£40-50/\$66-82.**

The buttoned flap was commonly known as 'the trap door'.

AN UNDERSKIRT (posh top petticoat) with vertical stripes of black and white silk woven with alpaca (quite stiff and springy to the touch) and hem flounces of horizontal stripes of black velvet bands on white. Drawstring ties pull in the fullness at the back. The underskirt is both machine and hand sewn. Mostly in good condition, some repair. This is a very chic and attractive garment. The Victorians loved really eye-catching underskirts; all that lifting the skirt business to go upstairs or step into a carriage. La! – there might have been a man watching, and he needed to be and was entertained. 1895-1900. **£80-100/\$132-165.** (See also front jacket illustration.)

CHEMISE (the basic undergarment), knee length, made from extremely fine cotton lawn, sleeveless, with wide, deep, ribbon drawstring neckline, edged with lace. There are true lovers' knots made from inserted lace decorating the top of this chemise. All hand sewn. Very pretty, very feminine and wearable now as a nightie. About 1892. **£80-90/$132-148.**

DRAWERS, full, wide, lace flounced and be-ribboned, made from fine cotton lawn. They have two separate legs, completely open, for 'convienience', except for a few inches attached at the centre front. They gather up on a drawstring (which is how drawers got their name) but, to modern minds, these are incredibly rude knickers! This pair is sumptuous, completely hand wrought. Both the chemise and drawers once belonged to an English countess (as part of her wedding trousseau) and they boast her entwined married initials embroidered at the front. Such rapture. 1892. **£80/$132.**

VIP's underclothes were usually made in sets, anything from 6 to 100.

ANOTHER PAIR of drawers made from fine linen, this time plain as a pikestaff but with hand sewing that makes you weep for its beauty. Wide, separate legs, decorated with four rows of pin tucks; small linen button at back overlap, drawstring waist. This is altogether a very prosaic pair of knickers in a pattern that would not have changed for sixty years, but the one difference with this pair is that they belonged to Queen Victoria. A teeny-weeny crown and 'VR' are embroidered on the waistband – plus the set number, 25. They measure 48½ inches around the waist! And to think that this pair might have sat on the throne in about 1890. Their value is anyone's guess, but probably about **£200-300/$330-500.**

> *Actually, I've done quite a study of old knickers: they're my thing and I wrote a book about them. All hell was let loose at the vicarage because these smalls (some of them very large) used to appear all over the house when I was researching their history. The vicar was not amused.*

CORSET MADE FROM a heavy-duty material called 'coutil', black, woven with red. The corset has 22 bones and is machine sewn and hand finished. Original stay-lace. (Stays was another word for corset.) Not as posh as some, but a much older pattern, with curved front busk and lots of inserted gussets to support the bust and allow for the fullness of the hips. This hefty corset was made for a big lady, possibly a size 16 who grew into a size 18! Inside the fawn, cotton twill lining, written in ink, is a note: 'Mrs. Peglar – 5 inches larger'. You can see where the *corsetière* has had to insert the extra material into the sides. The condition is middling to good. About 1900. **£85-90/$140-150**.

The corset was worn over the chemise and the drawers. Corsets can be difficult to date accurately as the styles were slow to change. The ones I describe are from the late nineteenth century and were doubtless worn for ages afterwards (especially when they got 'comfy').

BLACK, SATINIZED COTTON corset, lined in white glazed cotton, with 22 whalebones, which, on the outer side, are over-cased with strips of tan leather, back laced and with a straight-fronted, shaped steel centre-busk (the bit where the hooks and eyes do up) marked 'Coach Spring'. This would have been used by a curvey size 14 and would have clinched her into a nicely packed size 12. It is machine sewn and it's decorated with a bit of black lace, tacked along the top edge. Stamped inside the lining: 'The Celebrated DERMATHISTIC Corset. REGD' (the Victorians loved medical-sounding names) 'QUALITY 1'. In other words, this was a special buy. About 1890. **£100-150/$165-248**.

The first sewing-machines imported to this country went to the corset trade because, as you can imagine, the hand sewing was extremely hard graft.

A 'GREENERY-YALLERY' dress inspired by the Aesthetic Movement. Known to me as Sarah Bernhardt, the dress has lots of 'aesthetic' elements that make it interesting as a collectable. Designed as a one-piece Princess line, this dress is predominantly soft woollen cloth, shaded in bands of mushroom and brick-dust pink (Lucifer) with huge 'bishop' sleeves ending in a frilled cuff. The front panel, cut as an all-in-one underskirt, is quilted satin and the bodice has a high neck and shawl collar in bronze green (Florentine) velvet. The train of the dress starts at the neck and, gathering fullness, extends into the skirt in an eighteenth-century manner. Fully lined, with internal pocket, 12 cased bones and a stay-strap, it front fastens with hooks and eyes. Unmarked, dressmaker made. Machine and hand finished. It is a fascinating

The Princess line was popularized by Alexandra, Princess of Wales, in the 1870s.

informal dress, or 'tea gown', vaguely like a housecoat of the 1950s. Victorian/Edwardian, middle- or upper-class women, having loosed their stay-laces, 'lounged' in these frocks (before getting tightened up again for dinner) yet would be happy to receive *lady* callers for tea... and probably give them a bit of Elizabeth Barrett Browning to go with the sandwiches. The dress, although uncommon, is in poor condition – torn, moth holes, etc. Nothing that a few days intensive care and a specialist clean won't improve, but it does affect the price. **£70-90/$115-148**.

SPLENDID Arts and Crafts button-through smock-frock of embroidered linen – decidedly aristocratic rather than peasant. About 1900. **£120-150/$198-248**. Lovely, mauvey-purple cashmere robe, like a medieval scholar's gown, with huge bishop's sleeves. The front, shoulders and cuffs edged with wide bands of violet velvet and subdued, bronze braid. It's very theatrical – Portia in *The Merchant of Venice* – beautifully made and doubtless at one time would have been worn with a matching dress. A bit moth-eaten, but still smashing. Both about 1890. **£80-100/$132-165**. (*See Plate 2.*)

IN BRISKER, holiday mood, the next outfit is a jolly two-piece in heavy cotton, woven in broad panels of navy blue and white vertical stripes with contrasting areas of fine check. It has a bolero jacket, cut with masculine-looking revers and a walking-length skirt. I adore this outfit. You imagine her, striding along the sea-front at Eastbourne, complete with parasol and straw boater. It is very chic, simple and elegant. Entirely machine sewn, with internal back pocket, it is beautifully tailored and, I feel (sadly no label), probably French. Worn with a high-necked white blouse and a silver belt (see below) it looks, and must always have looked, stunning. About 1895. **£150/$248**.

Capes were often made from a circle of broad-loomed, felted wool with a cut up the front.

THREE-QUARTER-LENGTH cape in cream felt, decorated with a shoulder cape of felt and heavy lace, with collar and buttons trimmed in russett velvet. Nothing epitomizes the new woman of the end of the nineteenth century better than the cape. There is something excitingly romantic about this dashing garment. It was elegant and practical, its name denoting the extra layers over the shoulders, whereas a mantle was a single layered garment. Marvellous to feel those swishing weighty folds. Condition good. 1890-1900. **£100-150/$165-248.** (*See Plate* 2.)

SHOES

What did ladies wear on their feet in the 1890s? Well, they wore all kinds of shoe and boot styles. Northampton was the centre of the trade in this country but London, Paris and Florence produced beautiful shoes as well. Collectable period shoes can be hard to find because, like now, they wore out and were quickly discarded. Most likely you will find evening shoes (which didn't get quite such hard wear) and the tougher boots or strong shoes.

Dark bronze kid court shoes with 1¾-inch Louis heel with long front tabs and (pointed) toes decorated with bronze beadwork buckles and bronze spangles. This is an afternoon into evening shoe. Shaped for left and right feet (not done before about 1865), size 5, but very narrow. No maker's label (possibly bespoke). Original price, 11/6d, marked on the sole. In good condition. Very Gwendoline. About 1895. **£60-70/$100-115.** (*See Plates* 2 *and* 7.)

Court shoes always have high heels and for centuries were de rigueur when you attended Court.

Fine black calf, 14-holed, long tabbed, lace-up boots with brogued, pointed toe-cap in the Oxford style and small, stacked heels. Superb craftmanship. About a size 4. Maker's name in gold lettering around the inside cuff: 'ANGEL 6 Rue Du 29 Juillet, Paris'. Condition middling to good. About 1890. **£50-60/$82-100.** (*See also Plate* 2.)

STOCKINGS AND GARTERS

I'm going to skip stockings in the 1890s and do them in the 1900s, since the style doesn't change that much. Suffice to say, they were made from cotton, silk or wool and, sometimes, for evening, were very colourful and exotic (embroidered snakes, birds and butterflies were popular, but you needed to be wealthy or an actress to indulge such taste). Lots of black was worn, or black with a white 'shoe' bit, because the dye ran and stained your feet. But another interesting and rare collectable is the garters that held stockings up. They can be plain, saucy or grandly decorated (for evenings or weddings). I adore garters and they have a fascinating history all of their own.

HATS

A huge assortment of millinery was available in all shapes and sizes and at all prices in the 1890s. There were thousands of little hat shops up and down the country and all the big department stores sold hats. Luton and surrounding towns in Bedfordshire were the centre of the straw hat industry. The hat was seen as the insignia of emancipation; older ladies wore bonnets, the 'Votes for Women' freedom fighters wore hats! It's nice if you can find hats with the makers' labels inside, and if they are in their original boxes, so much the better. By the way, always store your hats crown down, with plenty of tissue paper, one only to each box if possible.

FINE MAUVE STRAW HAT, 3-cornered 'marquise' shape (the masculine element was often evident in the 1890s, with sailor hats, trilbies and tricornes), trimmmed with curling, mauve ostrich feather and small purple and mauve flowers around crown and at the back. Black silk lining, with embroidered label: 'Woollands Bros, 1, 2, 3, 4, 5, 6, & 7, Lowndes Terrace, London'. In original plain oval box. A delightful, well-made hat, possibly worn for half-mourning in the late nineteenth century. Condition good. About 1898. **£100/$165.**

They liked everything but the kitchen sink on their hats.

ROUGH-PLAITED 'fancy' straw hat, with widest part of brim (3½ inches) set front. Decorated with frills of see-me-through chiffon, cream silk rosette, bits of lace and a clump of tatty silk flowers. It would have been skewered on with a hat-pin. Lined with silk, but no label. Condition good but a bit crushed. **£30-35/$50-60.**

TINY, WIRED BONNET (5 inches across) decorated with coils of black chenille and silver thread, sequins and navy velvet bows and tie-strings (it's always called a bonnet when it ties). White aigrette at front and two pale blue flowers to one side. Good condition. No label to bonnet but in original box, marked 'Low & Peebles, Milliners, Costumiers, and General Drapers, 18, St. John Street, PERTH'. 1890. **£70/$115 upwards.**

VERY NARROW, short, cream kid gloves, 3 buttoned, with 3 embroidered black 'spines' down the back. Possibly used for half-mourning (after a person died, the rule was that you wore total black for a designated time and then 'slighted' your mourning to become less wholly black). The gloves are machine and hand sewn. Stamped inside: 'Made in France (size 5¾)'. £12/$20.

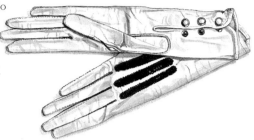

ANOTHER PAIR OF CREAM KID, bracelet-length gloves, with three brass button closure. They are decorated with fawn silk embroidery on the spines. Entirely hand sewn. Stamped inside: 'Ganterie de Luxe J. LANG Fabricant, Paris. (Size 6¼)'. £20/$33.

At a party, you would keep your gloves on to eat tiny cakes.

PUTTING ON YOUR GLOVES

Rich Victorian women wore exquisite gloves. The finest silk, coolest cotton, softest suede and kindest kid leather were used to make gloves to cover delicate hands. A lady (whether she was or no) always aspired to have tiny hands, the trademark of a superior person; thus upper- and middle-class ladies squeezed their hands into narrow gloves that, if well made, gently confined and flattered the natural shape.

Gloves could be helped on by having a bit of French chalk sprinkled into them and by getting the maid to ease them gently with glove stretchers, which are themselves interesting to collect.

The best gloves were made abroad, particularly in France, since the French understood the subtlties of how women dressed – a heady mix of display, flirty sophistication and sensuality. However, extremely nice gloves were made in Britain, too. Colours were 'quiet' cream, grey, fawn, bronze, black for funerals and white for weddings. Short and long (3 or 4 buttoned) for day and long (up to 10 buttons) for evening. The button hook was one of the most overworked devices in a Victorian or Edwardian household.

Although originally many of these gloves would have been kept in special glove containers, I'm happy to keep mine, colour coded, in old shoe boxes, which protect them adequately enough.

HANDBAGS

In their gloved hands, ladies held fans (which developed a large spread in the 1890s to offset the width of the sleeves) and handbags.

Now, I love bags and purses. I think they are such an essential part of women's dress. It's no use explaining to a man that a handbag contains *your life*, every item vital, as they have no understanding of this. Certainly, women have been carrying bags for a few hundred years; and, no wonder, because most often on a family outing they get given everyone else's stuff to put in them.

1890s ladies had some attractive and interesting bags. They still used professionally embroidered evening purses and homemade 'Dorothy' bags, but they also travelled on steam trains with sturdy, rather masculine, leather 'handbags' (filled to the brim with all the paraphernalia likely to be needed *en route*).

I store handbags closed, with tissue paper inside and a peice of tissue wrapped around them, and keep them in deep boxes or cases. Occasionally, I might use one or two of the evening purses for parties.

A GILT-FRAMED, day handbag (8 × 5 inches) made from violet ruched satin and velvet, decorated with gilt bosses and pieces of mother-of-pearl, opening with a push-down clasp. Lined with violet silk, the single handle also bound in velvet, with gilt rings. An elegant bag, like a miniature 'Gladstone', its only function was to carry visiting cards, a lace hanky and smelling-salts. No label, but probably French. About 1895. **£70/$115**. (*See Plate 1*.)

A NOTHER METAL-FRAMED bag (7 × 5 inches), made from wine red plush and leather, with several compartments lined in red satin. The bag has a single, plush handle and slide-catch fastening. It is part a *necessaire* (complement of button-hook, manicure things, mirror, scissors, thimble and sewing bits in one side) and a pocketbook (calling cards, notebook, pencil, room for your love letters, money on the other side). Again, no label or manufacturer's stamp (always so frustrating), but a lovely, if weighty, piece. About 1890. **£20/$33**.

All sorts of metal 'mesh' purses were made at the end of the nineteenth century, from fine gold and silver to baser metals.

S MALL (4 × 4 inches) novelty purse made from chain-link metal, with a draw-chain handle. It is unusual because on one side there is a moulded brass medallion in the shape of a cat's face, complete with green glass eyes. No label (possibly German). About 1890. **£30/$50**.

THIS IS ONE of my favourite bags. I like it because it is simple, well crafted and timeless. It is a satchel of brown leather (probably pig-skin), measuring 6 × 6 inches, on a leather shoulder strap. The leather-cased frame opens at the top with a press-down catch (which also locks with a key) into an expanding interior. There's also a wallet compartment on the outside front, secured by another small catch. No label, apart from 'IIL' marked on the inside frame. I'd love to think it was made by Hermès, but I doubt it. Yet it shouts quality. 1895-1900. £100/$165.

BELTS

Around their waists, late nineteenth-century girls wore sensational belts, and sometimes attached their chatelaine purses to them. The belts could be made from any material – fabric, leather or metal – with large, ornamental, central buckles. The butterfly was a popular device and, as the Art Nouveau influence increased, other naturalistic flora or fauna subjects became fashionable.

SAGE GREEN LEATHER belt with large, swirly, brass centre buckle, back fastening with another clasp made of brass. Inside (and this is interesting) is a piece of elastic, attached end to end, with 'The COURT Patented Expanding Belt' printed on it. Obviously this helped with the desired grip-me-tight look – especially when a lady was riding a bike! About 1895. £12/$20.

A LINK BELT MADE from shaped, plated silver plaques, pierced in a medieval design; the back clasped by an extending chain and more plaques. These are not uncommon; uncomfortable to wear, they look a million dollars. Made in Birmingham. £65-70/$108-115. *(See Plate 2.)*

A BELT MADE FROM 2-inch wide metal thread ribbon in shades of gold, silver and mauve, with a 3-inch central ornament of stamped, gilded metal in the stylized form of a winged insect – and the clasp at the back is the same. Fair condition. A good example of the Art Nouveau style influencing accessories. About 1890. £25/$40.

UMBRELLAS AND SUNSHADES

As I was searching round the Costume Room for examples of the 1890s, I spied the Brolly Box in one corner. The umbrella and sunshade were natural accessories for a genteel Victorian woman: they were shields against that which threatened her most vital attraction, a fair complexion. She did not wish to be a sun-burnt, windswept girl of nature; she was a refined creature, created with care. Coarseness of any kind was abhorrent to her.

T HE TINY, FRINGED parasol had been out of fashion for some thirty years when this one was made in the 1890s. Cream cotton overlaid with net covered with appliquéd muslin flowers and bows. The shaft and hooped handle made from polished wood, imitating bamboo. It has a metal frame and is 37 inches long. When open, it has a pleasing dome shape. Re-covered (they often are), but a good example of its kind. About 1890. **£25/$40.**

H ERE IS AN umbrella-cum-sunshade that remains one of my most loved possessions. Strong black silk, that furls tightly, sewn to a Fox & Co 'Paragon' frame. The robust shaft, 36 inches to the ferrule, is Malacca. The treat is a delightful, novelty handle – a lamb's head, cast in metal, with brown

glass eyes and long ears, that, at the touch of a button on the shaft, spring outward at the same time as the lamb's mouth opens to reveal a pink tongue and two teeth. There is a brass mount at the lamb's neck on which the original owner's initials 'I.H.' are engraved, as is the maker's name, Brigg & Co., a famous umbrella/walking-stick shop in Piccadilly (now in Old Bond Street) that specialized in amusing handles. About 1898. **£100-150/$165-248.**

Here I must stop to put all these things away and get out the next load – and, since I'm the 'in-house vicar' for the day, try and sort out a few parish problems: someone's lost the key to the organ loft, an American couple called and wanted information about a 'fore-bear' who's possibly buried in our churchyard, there are twin babies wanting christening and a girl phoned to book the church for her wedding... in two years' time.

MEN'S ATTIRE OF THE 1890S

I don't specialize in men's clothes (please, don't let that put you off men or clothes, as they make an interesting study), and I have decided to show throughout the book the one male item I have consistently collected – underpants. Nothing, vouchsafe, could be more revealing about the true nature of the male image in the last hundred years than a reflective look at his smalls.

Men have worn underpants for hundreds and hundreds of years and in the nineteenth century they were called under-drawers or pantaloons. The best were made from silk, but, obviously, wool, flannel, cotton and linen (and other materials) were also used. Men's clothes, including their underclothes, changed very, very slowly during the nineteenth and early twentieth centuries, seemingly impervious to the throb and thrum that drove the band-waggon of women's fashion. Male clothes in general are not as easy to collect as women's clothes as there are fewer about, and one of the most impoverished areas of all is under-linen.

Lock-knit silk was exactly the material that Coco Chanel siezed on by 1920 to make women's clothes, after seeing her rich boyfriend sporting his undies.

ANKLE-LENGTH PANTALOONS (32-inch inside leg) in lock-knit silk, with reinforced crutch and back ties, threading through 3 sets of hand-sewn eyelet holes. The wide, 3-button waistband front has loops for braces (these slotted through the pants before buttoning onto the trousers). Very finely machine stitched with set number, 3, embroidered in red. Another label on the inside fly states 'Patent Star Seal' and gives both British and USA patent numbers.

UNDER-VEST IN BEAUTIFUL, cream, lock-knitted silk. It is sleeveless, long and front buttoning, like a shirt, and very neatly hand sewn. At the hem there is a 'w' woven into the material. This may denote the famous British socks and stockings company, 'Wolsey', since underwear made from loomed material is part and parcel of the hosiery industry. Both are in good condition. **£60-70 / $100-115 the pair.**

THE 1900s EDWARDIAN DELIGHTS

Was there ever a more beguiling time for women's dress than the start of the twentieth century? I doubt it. Fashionable Society women now dressed in a softer, flowing style, the fabrics generally more yielding than before, although the shape still dictated a very small waist to offset the bosom (which, when covered in frills and drapes, tended to overhang like a decorated balcony). The corset, whose business it was to create this effect was, in a word, masterly! By 1900, equipped with two suspenders, its straight-fronted design pushed the stomach flat, flung the bust forward and arched the back into an 'S'-bend. Thus, female hips were allowed to be expansive, cello-shaped, swathed in long skirts that usually displayed a wealth of exciting detail near the hem. Sleeves remained important – lavished with puff and ruffle – while underclothes, increasingly frilly, were wrought with large amounts of insertion lace, threaded with ribbons and fastened with tiny mother-of-pearl buttons.

The beginning of the century, for day and evening dress-up occasions, was enchanting and intensely feminine. Looking at photographs of High Society events of the early 1900s, it always appears to have been warm, sunny weather in which graceful, pale-garbed ladies drifted ceaselessly over well-kept lawns.

Evening parties during the Season sparkled with lustrous silks, lace and diamonds – and pearls, masses of pearls.

Clothes to make you gasp!

Within a few more years, this opulent look was to end and a distinctly more practical, utilitarian fashion could be observed, slowly advancing throughout all classes. If the first years of Edwardian fashion suggested a curve, from 1908 the vertical was more the mark. Women from every walk of life gradually adopted simpler, less fussy clothes and gained not only more comfort but, in many cases, a great deal more elegance by so doing.

Yet for costume collectors, the period can be a dry desert. For instance, the splendid trailing skirts were one of the first fashion casualties of domestic economy during the First World War – scissors sliced across their deep hems as skirts grew shorter – while boned bodices (which were old-fashioned and fitted no one once corsets loosened their grip) were stripped of their trimmings and confined to the rag-bag. However, you do find plenty of underwear, accessories and, surprisingly, quite a few dresses from the end of the decade, when the style had become classically slender and tubular. The other items to look out for are blouses, the fashion novelties of the early 1900s, some plain, some very elaborate.

CLOTHES OF THE 1900S

In many ways, at first glance, there doesn't seem to be much change in the general style of clothes between the 1890s and the 1900s. Rather, it tends to be the materials that reflect the new approach to dressing. By the way, always look out for original Society, fashion or women's magazines from any decade because often they can tell you more about what people wore than any costume book yet written.

> Since I'm writing this bit of the book during the winter and the Costume Room is freezing, I — and the dog, because he follows me everywhere — go up to search about and my fingers get so numb I can hardly hold the clothes. The dog (whom I suspect of hating costume even more than the vicar) sits with sad eyes imploring me to be done and get downstairs to the Aga. Cold is OK for costume just as long as it's not damp. Dog and I must therefore suffer.

The outer bolero was fashionable at this date.

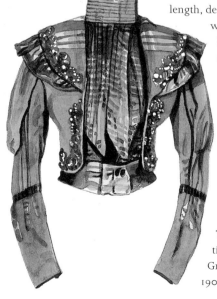

THIS OUTFIT IS MARVELLOUS because it is drop-dead smart. Superbly made, the bodice has an outer bolero and a collar edged with sparkling black sequins and jet beadwork, tailored over the integral black, tucked silk 'front' with its 2-inch high neck. The sleeves are full length, decorated with black satin 'strapwork', ending in tight cuffs. The bodice has a sewn-in satin belt that fits snug to the waist. Fully lined, with 12 cased whalebones, it front fastens with lots of hooks and eyes. The long skirt is plain, cut with a good 'swing' at the back and a front, side-placket fastening (big press studs); lined, it has two satin-edged frills at the hem. The embossed label on the stay-band reads: 'Ladies Tailors. Costumiers. D & A Prentice & Co., 24 Hamilton Street, Greenock'. It's absolutely lovely. 1900-05. £140/$230.

MOURNING DRESS

Because 1901 was the year of Queen Victoria's death, I thought I'd describe a funereal black two-piece. It is made from bombazine, a material associated with mourning for centuries before the Victorians got hold of it. Best quality bombazine is close woven from wool and silk and has no nap. It is very black, with no sheen – a proper cloth to display a depth of grief. At this date, as for centuries before, close female relatives in the first stage of bereavement had garments covered or banded in black crêpe (another significant mourning material), but after an appropriate period (ranging from weeks to several months), the mourning would be 'slighted', the crêpe lessened and a bit more decoration allowed. At least everyone knew what was going on! Every household in the land, even the poorest, would have had a bit of 'decent black' in the house – or could borrow some.

AN ITEM THAT EVERY sensible woman kept to hand: two 6-inch long, 'scissor'-type handles of plated metal that end with two facing leather discs, with a slide catch and a loop for cord slotted over the length. What can they be? Give up? They're skirt holders or 'lifters'. This nifty device, worn on an extended cord from your belt, gripped the hem of the skirt and hoisted it clear of the dirt when occasion demanded. I have two in the collection – both about 1900 (one is stamped 'The Tomatic' HK & Co.) and worked with swirly patterns. They are very collectable and, although mostly made from base metal, attractive. About 1900. £30/$50 upwards, depending on how ornate.

BLACK COSTUME

Now, beware! There are oceans of black turn-of-the-century clothes still around and they are not all 'mourning' outfits. Black was just very practical, especially for the working classes, so you are bound to find some black Victorian or Edwardian outer clothes in any case. Some of the stuff is reasonably priced – a few pounds – but some garments, like my two-piece described opposite, are immaculate, labelled and therefore more pricey.

The effect of the frills would give the required 'pouter pigeon' look to the bosom.

A$_\text{N}$ ELABORATE, BLACK NET blouse, with tiered frills, decorated with black velvet ribbon and 'spotted' chenille embroidery. The blouse has a 2-inch high choker collar and wide sleeves that have frilled 'Van Dycked' (in the style of dress of the seventeenth-century painter's portraits) points at the ends. The whole is lined with transparent cream 'illusion' (hardly there) silk. Hook-and-eye fastening at the back. A delicate, fancy affair, dress-maker made, that could be worn for afternoon (or informal evening) wear. In good condition, very wearable – and fairly rare. About 1900. **£90/$148.**

F$_\text{ROM}$ A FUNERAL to a wedding. A pretty, fussy, two-piece bridal dress of about 1908, made from soft, ivory-coloured silk satin, overlaid with net, lace and chiffon. It is most elaborate and, although damaged, still captures the heart with its charm. The back-fastened, blouse top (which has received most damage – someone has, literally, ripped its front

out) is designed with a high, boned collar and three-quarter length sleeves embroidered in floss-silk, with masses of 'ribbon-work' (scrolls of ribbon twisted into flower shapes and then appliquéd, by hand, onto the net). The skirt, 'gauged' (similar to smocking) to a fitted band, waist to hip, has plain, fluid, silk panels to the knee, where it fuses with net and becomes a riot of lace and trellised ribbon-work roses. It has further under-skirts of taffeta (now frail) and 'angel'-pleated chiffon. Machine and hand sewn. The original belt is missing. Label: 'Adele, 4 Hanover Street, London'. Poor condition. About 1908. **£40-50/$66-82.**

M$_\text{AROON}$ SILK UMBRELLA with swan's head handle sculpted in stained wood, complete with glass eyes. About 1900. **£50-60/$82-100.** *(See Plate 2.)*

S PEAKING OF ART NOUVEAU and all that 'organic' curve, I've just bought a lovely hair-pin from a local trash or treasure shop, totally in the style. Made from one wavy piece of 6½ inches of (imitation) tortoiseshell ending in a complicated serpentine loop. A really good example. **£7/$12.**

HAIR CURLERS

I've found a little box of steel 'curlers', well designed, with a round central bar that clips into a square frame. They are stamped on the side: 'Hindes, Lmd. Finsbury. London. E.C. Patent'.

Now, you may laugh, but 'Hindes' were the Rolls Royce of curlers and you see them advertised in all the best magazines at the turn of the century.

There are fourteen in this box, all working as well as the day they were made, so for sheer interest – and because this is exactly the sort of mundane object that is often thrown out and thus becomes rare – they have to be worth about **£10-15/$17-25**, if not more, to an early 'hair care' collector. They date from anywhere between 1900 and 1910.

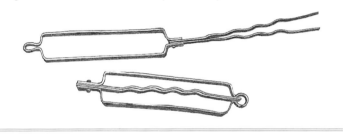

A BLOUSE MADE FROM soft, flesh-coloured pink satin, entirely hand sewn, and designed with cascades of half-inch tucks – front, back and sleeves (unbelievably difficult to do). There is a 3- to 4-inch high, boned choker and a 'vestee' (high-necked fill-in) front made from lace and net, with flat revers at the front decorated with swirls of Russian braid in exactly the same shade of pink. Fully lined in cream silk and fastening at the back with hooks and eyes and small pearl buttons. This is a work of such skill as to make you gasp. Probably French. Condition very good, apart from a few marks on one of the sleeves. About 1908. Unusual. **£90-100/$148-165.** (*See Plate 2.*)

Colour Plates

The clothes and accessories illustrated in the following colour plates are described in detail in the text entries listed below.

Plate 1: Handbags

FROM TOP, LEFT TO RIGHT:
Diamanté black bag, p.107, sixth entry; red leather bag, p.130, first entry; flat violet silk bag on ring handles with trailing wisteria and trims of fringe from about 1910; black and silver bag (corner shown), p.107, fifth entry; red 'Dorothy' bag, p.97, fifth entry; floral cocktail bag, p.111, first entry; biker bag with goggles, p.178, sixth entry; 'orb' bag, p.181, last entry; ruby red silk plush purse on ornate gilt frame from about 1890; purple bag, p.22, first entry.

Plate 2: 1890s and 1900s

ON DUMMIES, LEFT TO RIGHT:
First dummy: cloak, p.18, last entry; blouse, p.31, last entry. Second dummy: dress, p.37, first entry; parasol, p.49, first entry. Third dummy: suit, p.33, first entry; belt, p.23, third entry; purse, p.36, second entry. Fourth dummy: coat, p.18, second entry. Fifth dummy: suit, p.14, first entry.

ON STEPS IN FOREGROUND, LEFT TO RIGHT:
Umbrella, p.30, last entry; floral hat, p.40, last entry; black boots, p.19, third entry; boater, p.40, last entry; bronze shoes, p.19, second entry.

Plate 3: 1900s and 1910s

ON DUMMIES, LEFT TO RIGHT:
First dummy: black dress, p.52, last entry. Second dummy: pink dress, p.44, last entry. Third dummy: suit, p.47, third entry. Fourth dummy: dress, p.51, first entry.

ON STEPS IN FOREGROUND, LEFT TO RIGHT:
Black ankle-strap shoes, p.50, second entry; black laced shoes, p.50, third entry; black hat on stand, p.45, second entry; cream hat, p.40, second entry.

Plate 4: 1920s

ON DUMMIES, LEFT TO RIGHT:
First dummy and stand behind: wedding dress, p.58, first entry; head-dress and veil, p.58, second entry. Second dummy: dress, p.56, first

entry. Third dummy: suit, p.57, second entry. Fourth dummy: coat, p.57, first entry.

ON STEPS IN FOREGROUND, LEFT TO RIGHT:
Two-tone shoes, p.69, second entry; spotted scarf, p.73, first entry; hat box, p.65, first entry; snakeskin shoes, p.60, fourth entry; hat on stand, p.62, first entry.

Plate 5: 1930s

ON DUMMIES, LEFT TO RIGHT:
First dummy: coat, p.68, first entry. Second dummy: dress, p.68, second entry. Third dummy: dress and jacket, p.78, last entry. Fourth dummy: dress, p.77, last entry.

ON STEPS IN FOREGROUND, LEFT TO RIGHT:
Hat on stand, p.65, second entry; red shoes, p.70, first entry; straw hat, p.73, second entry; dressing case, p.70, last entry; gold shoes, p.79, second entry; silver and gold shoes, p.69, last entry.

Plate 6: 1940s

ON DUMMIES, LEFT TO RIGHT:
First dummy: suit, p.96, third entry; scarf, p.92, fourth entry. Second dummy: knitted jacket, p.97, third entry. Third dummy: dress, p.93, third entry. Fourth dummy: coat, p.96, first entry; scarf, p.98, 'Scarves' box.

ON STEPS IN FOREGROUND, LEFT TO RIGHT:
Brown shoes, p.89, fourth entry; red shoes, p.96, last entry; basket, p.92, second entry; brown shoes, p.91, fourth entry; tan hat, p.90, third entry; three remaining hats, p.91, second entry.

Plate 7: Shoes

FROM TOP, LEFT TO RIGHT:
White boots, p.131, fourth entry; red shoes, p.132, first entry; plastic shoes, p.178, second entry; flower sprigged (toe only), p.122, second entry; silver and gold (toe only), p.99, last entry; bronze (in box), p.19, second entry; pale pink (in box), p.36, second entry; diamanté heeled, p.50, second entry; tapestry boot (toe only), p.164, fifth entry; red lizard-skin, p.130, first entry; white flat shoes, p.98, first entry.

Bright blue, wool, 2-piece, tailor-made walking dress with 'midi' edge-to-edge jacket. The jacket has long sleeves and a sailor collar (faced with heavy cream lace); lined with black cotton, it is boned and has a self-colour, top-stitching decoration. The skirt, lined at the hem, has a centre-side placket fastening (huge press-studs and hooks), internal pocket the size of a golf bag and a wonderfully cut, 'fish-tailed' skirt whose weighted hem is also top-stitched. No label, and it may originally have had a waistcoat, but it looks marvellous worn over a crisp shirt, belted at the waist. About 1905. £100-125/$165-206. (See Plate 2.)

Change of scene. Bathing-dress in heavy red twilled cotton (like denim) edged with white braid. A 2-piece comprising Andy Pandy all-in-one trouser suit with full collar with 3 huge pearl buttons down a front opening. A separate, braided skirt with another button fastening is worn over the top. A tape inside gives the original owner, 'M.C. Hacon' and, marked in ink, 'Boston House'. Definitely not made for an Olympic swim, but so atmospheric you can almost smell the sea. Rather faded, but unusual, especially with the skirt. About 1900. £60-100/$100-165.

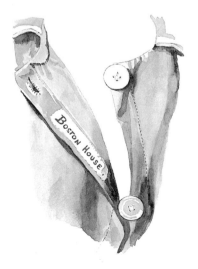

A WELL-TAILORED, tight-waisted jacket with deep peplum made from dark, aubergine-coloured face cloth, with 'pouched' front, velvet collar and large revers decorated with cream felt and braid in art nouveau style, repeated on the full sleeve cuffs. Although there are two decorative metal buttons, the jacket fastens with large hooks and eyes. Lined with cream silk (very fragile) with a worn label. The skirt is missing, so although a good example of its time, the price is modest. About 1900. **£35/$58.**

SHORTER THAN THE step-ins below, a pair of wonderful combinations in a fine, soft, plain weave cotton called nainsook, sleeveless and back-fastened with tiny pearl buttons (you'd need a maid to do them up). There are very full frills at the (split) leg ends (my tape-measure ran out at 60 inches and there was still another 10 to go) and the whole garment is a profusion of superlative hand-sewing. And, as if that wasn't enough, there are insertions of hand-made lace *and* amazing decorations done in drawn thread-work in a floral design of irises – what could be more 1900 arty than that? Probably made abroad, but don't ask me where. No label, but very grand – and more sexy than you'd believe. Wedding trousseau stuff. This pair are the Vincent Van Gogh of knickers. About 1900. **£150/$248 upwards.**

There are many such petticoats to be found, as every lady had one, but some are nicer than others.

TRADITIONAL WHITE COTTON petticoat with insertion lace banded from knee to hem, ending with a deep frill of machine lace. Tape ties and linen buttons at the back. Machine and hand sewn. Condition (good) important. About 1900. **£35-50/$58-82 upwards.**

SLEEVELESS, MID-CALF, white cotton combinations with vertical lace insertion throughout. No fastenings of any sort – you just stepped into the two legs (still split asunder) and yanked the rest up around you. Professionally hand sewn (all that female sewing labour still abounded). Excellent condition. About 1900. **£60-80/$100-132.**

A PAIR OF 'RATIONAL', boneless stays (the Reform Dress lobby swore by these). The shoulder-strapped corsets are made from tough, biscuit-coloured cotton (coutil), corded and seamed with a laced back (16 pairs of metal eyelet holes) with 8 buttons (on tape shanks) fastening the front. Pleated gussets over the bust. Beautifully designed and machine sewn. Three buttons at each hip (for button-on drawers/petticoat or early suspenders). Looks like a big girl's Liberty bodice. No label. Uncommon. About 1900. **£60-100/$100-165.**

The stays were always worn over the top of the 'combs'.

A ND, TO GO OVER IT, a 'spencer' – sort of 'underneath' cardigan (both garments named after peers of the realm). Close-fitting, natural wool jersey with long sleeves and set of small pearl buttons to front fasten. Manufactured. Dating from about 1910, but made for years before and after that date, for warmth. Label: 'Trade Mark (nice St. Bernard Dog logo) Alpine S & S'. Plus sewn on, paper retailer's label: 'Sam: Clappen, Drapery Dept. Cricklade Street, Cirencester. 5/11 and a half pence'. (These sort of labels are a bonus when collecting.) Good condition. **£15-20/$25-33.**

A NOTHER SPENCER, exactly the same shape, but with lace trimmed neck and sleeves, bearing the label: 'Aertex, The Cellular Cotton Company, London'. Retail label: 'Made In England. E. & H Deane. Outfitters. BATH'. The bodice is also in pristine condition (Aertex is very tough) and the Arbiter of Good Taste would wear it as a blouse, if I gave her half a chance. **£15-20/$25-33.**

Aertex was a resilient cotton material which was invented in 1887.

H ERE'S ANOTHER PRACTICAL ITEM – a handbag. Classic shape (12 × 8 inches), a frame bag in brown tooled and embossed leather with a single strap, sliding catch, lock and key. Inside lined with brown silk and fitted with pockets for an array of ladies' travelling necessities, including small, gilt topped glass bottles, (scent, brandy...?), brushes, comb, looking-glass, etc. All rather jolly. Fair to middling condition. About 1909. **£65/$108.**

HANDBAGS

Ladies' hand-held baggage was beginning to be known as just 'handbags' by the early 1900s, and there was a move towards large, capacious bags by the end of the century. As fashionable female clothes became distinctly slender in profile by 1908 (and therefore had no bulky pockets), these expanding carry-alls were an effective balance to the fashion for increasingly large hats.

R ATHER MORE IMPRACTICAL, except for carriage-calls, is an engraved, moulded, silver metal purse with small chain and 'finger loop' handle, which could also be clipped to a waist belt. These were very popular and considered genteel from the late nineteenth century into the Edwardian period. At 5 × 3 inches, this one is large enough for its green, watered silk lining to have held the all important visiting cards. Plate a bit worn. 1900. **£38/$62.** (*See also Plate 2.*)

D AINTY, PALE PINK SATIN (now very frail), elastic-sided, Louis-heeled, pointy evening shoes, with high, eighteenth-century style uppers, decorated with festoons of bronze beads. Gold embossed label: 'The London Shoe Company'. Ah, snooty shoes – in their day they must have been gorgeous. Sadly, too many dressing-ups since leave them worn out: aristocrats down on their uppers. About 1900. **£12-15/$20-25.** (*See also Plate 7.*)

These shoes are pictured to the right above.

P AIR OF DARK BROWN, calf leather and suede, brogued, lace-up shoes with squat Louis heels and pointed toes. Label: 'Taylor & Son. Makers. 82 Portland Street, London'. Missing laces, but with original 'Selby Adjusting Shoe Tree' inside. About 1905, and forever in fashion afterwards. **£45/$75.**

SHOE PARAPHERNALIA

While we're about it, other collectable items asoociated with shoes are shoe-horns and button-hooks. Sometimes you find them with very decorative handles in all sorts of materials – from precious metals to horn and wood – or you can find them, like mine, as a sturdy 'combo' made of polished steel with a plain ivory handle. The more decorative and pretty the handles, the more expensive the item.

This is a steel and ivory button-hook, shutting down to a neat eight inches against the horn when not in use. This was probably designed for a man (it seems to be too robust for a lady), but it's still beautifully made. About 1900. £23 / $40.

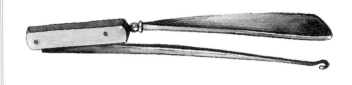

A SIMPLE, SLENDER SUMMER DRESS of white cotton gauze with 3-inch high neckline (supported by wire spirals). Three-quarter length sleeves 'cut in one' with the bodice. Deliciously ornamented with heavy, art nouveau motifs embroidered in mauve and with vermicelli wiggles of white silk braid. Professionally hand sewn (tons of intricate work – back to faggoting, etc.), fastened at the back (fetch the maid...) with buttons and hooks and eyes. An understated dress, its simple fabric and style belying the sophistication of the design. It has a strange little label at the waist – interwoven 'v's with a '46'. I sense that it originated in Paris. 1908-10. £200-£300 / $330-500 and upwards. (*See Plate 2.*)

Paul Poiret, the dress designer, revived this classical 'Empire' look by 1907.

H EAVY SILK EMBROIDERED, late afternoon or evening purse (7 × 9 inches), bronze overall but with a pattern of pink roses. Lined in leaf green silk and set on a curved, chased gilt metal frame with push-down catch and chain handle. This little bag would still look lovely for a party today. Condition very good. 1900-10. £75-80 / $120-132.

BEAD BAGS

If in perfect condition, a good beaded or silk embroidered bag of the period could be worth upwards of £100/$165 – the more fancy the beadwork or larger the purse the more they cost.

Professionally beaded or embroidered purses were always expensive items when new. Bead and embroidered bags are vulnerable and often get damaged. Look after them carefully – they are worth it.

A PAIR OF BLACK AND MAUVE cotton 'mourning' stockings with four wide 'clocks' (vertical, arrowhead decorations, ankle to calf). A bit faded, with two big darns at the welt (the metal suspender clips must have cut through), but a nice example of Edwardian hosiery. 1900-10. £10/$17.

A CORSET, REALLY MORE A 'WASPIE', 10 inches in depth, made from strong white cotton with 28 cased whalebones and a sturdy steel 'busk' down the front, with big lachets and studs. It is laced at the back and has 2 long suspenders (buckled at 13 inches, but they could extend to 20 to accommodate hose which was often quite short in the leg) with handsome, art nouveau, metal clips worked with a sliding stud. This is definitely intended for a young thing whittling her waist down to the required 21 inches. It's in very good condition and fairly unusual (they mostly got chucked away). About 1900. £120/$198.

P AIR OF PALE, creamy pink silk stockings with embroidered arrowhead clocks from the ankle. The initial 'M' (Morley, the makers) woven at the welt. Good condition. 1900-09. £20/$33.

N OW HERE'S A FETCHING pair of pantaloons – knickers – made in baby pink striped silk of the sheerest kind, measuring 27 inches from (ah-ha) *elasticated* waist to *elasticated* knees, hand sewn, trimmed with pale pink ribbon rosettes and altogether glorious. She must have looked divine in these. Worn under the 'hobble skirt', these are true 'Directoire'-style knickers – the sort my mother and grandmother used to speak of in hushed tones. Rare early bloomers. About 1909. £50/$82.

MODESTY COVERS

On a 'they don't do that anymore' note, if you had a personal maid, even up to the 1950s, in households where the mistress's clothes were 'put ready', the intimate apparel was always discreetly veiled (*a man* might see it) with modesty covers – usually charmingly embroidered or decorated. Funnily enough, lots of erstwhile knicker covers ended up as pram covers!

S PLENDID MODESTY COVER in cream satin with a quilted lining, edged with silk cord, 22 inches by 26 inches, part of a wedding trousseau for a bride and adorned with her espoused initials, I.A.B. (Ida Atherton Brown), and a big satin bow on the corner. About 1907. To me absolutely priceless, but they are around – from a few pounds to a lot more if they're very ooh-la-la.

N ATURAL WOOL FLANNEL PETTICOAT, mid-calf length, neatly handsewn to a cotton hip yoke, edged with knitted 'Shetland' lace, with tie tapes and a linen button fastening at the back. This style of winter warmer just went on and on, from early centuries until people started to live in hotter houses. It might date from the 1880s but I bet it was worn well into the twentieth century. It's in good condition (no moths — and they like nothing better than a bit of flannel to chew on) and fairly rare, especially with the lace. **£25-35/$40-58** upwards.

L ARGE-BRIMMED, LIGHTWEIGHT ladies' *sola topee* (pith helmet — *sola* is a tropical swamp plant, the pith of which insulates the headgear) covered in fine white cotton and lined with dull green cloth. Label: 'Ramsey & Co. Contractors. Bangkok. By appointment'. This came to me in a tin hat box along with a gauzy mosquito veil that had, presumably, been worn with it. About 1900. **£50/$82**. *(See Plate 3.)*

H ATS GREW EXTRAVAGANTLY LARGE at the end of Edward VII's reign — worn over piles of hair, secured by vast hat pins. I have one in sea-blue straw, the crown alone measuring 9 inches across, brim to brim 20 inches, caught up on one side by a blue ostrich feather and a few battered violas. Lined with black silk, the gold label reads 'Court Milliner. *Valerie* New Burlington St.' About 1910. **£65/$108**.

V ERY LARGE, FIRM STRAW hat in a boater style, decorated with an abundance of violets and pale mauve satin ribbon. Label: 'Excelsior'. About 1910. **£80-100/$132-165**. And a small cream straw boater with traditional striped silk band. 1900-10. **£25-30/$40-50**. *(See Plate 2.)*

MILLINERY

It is a charming fact that wealthy, married gentlemen in the eighteenth, nineteenth and early twentieth centuries often established their lady-friends with small millinery businesses in a fashionable part of town. These establishments were respectable, discreet — and nice little earners.

MEN'S UNDERWEAR OF THE 1900S

A PAIR OF CHAMOIS LEATHER men's underpants. Absolutely fabulous. Machine and hand sewn (lots of patches to make them fit) with top button fly fastening and tape loops for the braces. They are now 'trunks' but I'm certain that when new they would have been breeches – someone has cut the knee bands off. However, they are lucky to be here at all; I was given them by a lady who told me that they, and others like them, had belonged to her late father-in-law but, gradually, they had been utilized by the family as car and window wash cloths. The late nineteenth century advertised 'chammy' leather under-drawers for both sexes as being beneficial to health and excellent 'when in the saddle'. Unique. About 1900. I have never seen another pair, so can only guess their value, **perhaps £30-50 / $50-82.**

1910-1920 THE LAST DAYS OF OLD FROCKS

We now approach some of the most rewarding years for a costume historian. The second decade of the century was to prove a strange, transitional time, especially for women; and, not surprisingly, you see this reflected in what was worn. Class boundaries began to crumble as better educated, working-class women actively sought new jobs outside the home and during the First World War bravely took on heavy, erstwhile 'male' jobs on the home front. 'Society' women, with their luxurious clothes, still survived, but by the end of this decade more clothes, even 'dressy' clothes, were being bought or made and worn by ordinary women.

London boasted fine department stores: Selfridges opened its doors in 1909 and its advertising, according to a caption writer of the day, was 'conducted on a scale of unexampled magnitude'. Further along Oxford Street were D. H. Evans (1879), Peter Robinson (1833) and Bourne and Hollingsworth (moved here in 1902). Dickens & Jones (earlier,

Dickens & Smith) moved to Regent Street in 1835, and Harrods, grandest of all, had started trading in Knightsbridge in 1849. All these stores relied heavily on the capricious whims of Dame Fashion to boost their profits. Enormous numbers of clothes must have been sold from these great shops.

As we have seen, many fine nineteenth-century clothes went under the scissors because of War shortages and were re-made in 'newer' styles. Therefore, in general, completely original clothes, especially top clothes, from about 1913-18 are not abundant – but don't let that stop you looking, because it is a fascinating ten years. Do read all you can about the decade and look at other decorative arts so that you can feel their influence on fashion styles.

Contemporary books and old magazines that deal with women's lives and clothes are enchanting. One of my favourites is Flora Klickmann's *Needlework Economies: A Book of Making and Mending with Oddments and Scraps* of 1919. It is a treasury of homely advice about how to make a pair of bloomers from the legs of old winter stockings; how to keep out the wind with a patchwork of cast-off kid gloves sewn onto a flannel undervest; and, fascinatingly, guidance on making 'the new' brassière from half a yard of material and a little Irish crochet work. As a costume collector, this is the sort of riveting information you will be eager to tuck under your belt.

CLOTHES 1910-1920

One of the remarkable aspects of collecting clothes and storing them is the charming smell they have. I mean it! People always imagine that

> *I love my collection of old clothes; indeed, to tell the truth, they are probably more fussed over than my personal wardrobe.*

old clothes smell bad, but I can assure you that mine don't. These smell gorgeous: when you open the door of the Costume Room you are assailed by a heady aroma, a fragrant mix of washing powder, old scent, moth balls and pot pourri sachets. I store the old linen in cases with lavender bags.

Stiff, turn-of-the-century, usually lining silks tend to have a degenerate quality and rarely survive in good condition.

TWO-PIECE AFTERNOON DRESS or costume in lavender ribbed silk, the bodice with a high collar, 10 cased bones, front fastening with hooks and eyes. It has bracelet-length sleeves trimmed with pleated organza and self-cloured velvet ribbons. The skirt is long but straighter than previously fashionable, and has 2 deep, vertical tucks, waist to hem, decorated with self-coloured embroidered French knots and large buttons. Fully lined – although the skirt lining is 'shattering'. Superbly tailored, machine and hand sewn. It's a slightly old-fashioned dress for a mature lady and it reminds me of those photographs of H.M. Queen Mary. Gold embossed label on stay-strap: 'Joseph Beckett, Eastgate Row, Chester'. Apart from the lining, it's in very good order – and a pretty colour. About 1910. **£150/$248**.

A PETTICOAT (that goes with the above dress) made from firm silk, with elasticated waist and side hooks and eyes. Decorated for 20 inches from hem in bands of lace, puffed chiffon, pink ribbon and, sewn on at intervals, small pink chiffon 'roses' with green ribbon leaves. It's attractive. About 1910. **£40-50/$66-82**.

IN CONTRAST, THE 'ARABIAN LOOK', what a 25 year-old daughter might have worn. Bright, sugar pink, soft silk satin dress in a close-fitting style – the skirt a tad towards 'hobble'. The bodice is worked on a structured but not boned cotton lining which closes at the front. The outer, pretty, lace vestee front then poppers together over that and the all-in-one sleeves (magyar) end with a frill of lace to match. As decreed by avant-garde dress designers of this period (Poiret, Lucile and the like), the skirt is slit to the knee (to get a glimpse of the underskirt... shades of the harem) and caught up with a pink cabbage rose and a bunch of silk bobbles. Lots of things to 'do up': 24 press-studs, plus 9 hooks and eyes, not including those on the black velvet sash. No label; dress-maker made. Very good condition. 1910-12. **£60-80/\$100-132; £100/\$165 plus if it had a label.** (*See Plate 3.*)

Afternoon and evening wear for young women sought a look of deceptive spontaneity (slightly theatrical, 'dragged from the slave-market') which, in practice, was most contrived.

THE SORT OF LARGE HAT (the silhouette was 'T' shape) that might well have been worn with either the above dress or with the brown suit on page 47. Cat-black velvet, 27 inches overall, with vast domed crown — but the brim beginning now to slope downward. Lined in black cotton. No label. 1910-12. **£65/\$108 upwards.** (*See Plate 3.*)

HAT DECORATIONS

Remember to look out for hat decorations — feathers (but, thank heaven, by 1912, a few people were beginning to campaign against the wholesale slaughter of exotic birds for their plummage) and ribbons, exquisite ribbons, all of dazzling quality. Also watch out for large hat pins, 12 inches and more. They're much collected nowadays — there's even a Hat Pin Society — but you can still find pins, best in pairs or boxed, at reasonable prices. Just make sure they're not faked up, old buttons or brooches soldered onto modern pins. Most of all, I enjoy hat brooches, which are very large, rather showy, but fairly light, with big pins at the back. Butterflies, birds, dragonflies are popular designs. **£15/\$25 upwards, depending on style, material and condition.**

BRASSIÈRE, MANUFACTURED FROM white cotton and 'curtain' lace with tie tapes (that cross at back and tie in front) and one button. Label: 'Venus Brassiers. Guaranted [*sic*] Hand made. Bust 40'. 1914-20. **£15-25/\$25-40.**

THE BRASSIÈRE

The brassière came into being about 1907-14. It was derived from the camisole, which, as the corset began to slip downwards and become a girdle, turned into a bust-bodice, a garment that my old aunts always called, enigmatically, 'B-Bs' – and for years I thought this was something to do with paying guests. However, commercially, the bust-bodice, fairly soon after 1907, began to be known as a brassière.

Its success didn't happen overnight, and there were (and are still) hundreds and thousands of women who never wore the wretched things *ever*. But lots of younger women didn't want to wear rigid corsets under the softer dresses, so lighter, prettier, more practical undies begin to sweep in during this decade. And they were here to stay.

PAIR OF CREAM COTTON (jean cloth) stays, laced, whale-boned and steel busked, starting under the bust and extending to low over the hips in a much straighter design. This corset has other excitements – a sextet of suspenders. Marked inside 'Made in Canada', these were worn by a 1912 bride in that country. She must have clanked a bit when she walked down the aisle, but at least her stockings were probably wrinkle free. Bought complete with the 2-piece wedding dress, which was beautifully homemade and embroidered, for **£160/$264**.

A HOMEMADE CAMISOLE of white cotton, hand sewn with yoke and straps of dense crochet work. Tie tapes at neck and waist; linen button closure. About 1910. £15-20 / $25-33.

'Corset cover' is another old name for camisole.

B UST-BODICE, manufactured in strong cotton, with boned struts at back and seamed criss-cross support pieces. Front buttoning with tape and stay hook at waist. Stamped inside: 'Made for Pettit's, Kensington'. About 1915. £15 / $25.

H EAVY, DARK BROWN FLANNEL walking costume with trims of black braid. Three-quarter length jacket cut straight to below the hips, lined, with 3-button fastening and black silk facings on the long lapels. Skirt, fully lined, cut to ankle with broad panels of vertical braiding to match jacket. Label (in back of jacket): 'The Lilliputian Warehouse. W. Hayford and Sons, 204-205 Sloane St. London. By Royal Appointment' (retailer). Another: 'Marie et Cie. 18 St. Ann's Square, Manchester' (dress-maker). Extremely smart. A classic suit, size 14, good condition: you could wear it now. 1910-12. £175-200 / $288-330. (*See Plate 3.*)

L ONG-LINE, 'PROFESSOR HIGGINS' cardigan, or 'Ladies' Sports Coat' manufactured from a spun silk yarn in a ribbed design of blue and gold with collar, facings and turn-back cuffs in plain blue. Two pockets and 7 large mother-of-pearl buttons. It was worn, for many a long year, by a friend's mother when playing golf. It was this sport that started off ladies' keen desire to have comfortable, flexible, but elegant garments to wear when active. In fairly good condition, too. No label. Interesting and uncommon (most early knitwear has either worn away, been gobbled by moths or been chucked out). About 1910. £40-50 / $66-82 upwards.

Spun silk yarn could be artificial by this date.

GLOVE STRETCHERS

Don't forget glove stretchers, will you? This is another of those implements that proliferated in nineteenth- and early twentieth-century households. The pair I'm looking at are very common-place – 6 inches of smooth ivory (could be imitation) and used for the tiniest of gloves. Sometimes they come in sets of Large, Medium and Small (with the 'puffer' to blow the French chalk into the fingers) and can be found with silver, mother-of-pearl, ebony or other choice materials for their handles. Usually, the plainer and finer, the earlier they are. My pair is worth about £10 / $17. (*See also box on p.21.*)

P AIR OF GLOVES in fawn kid skin, with cuffs decorated with panels of darker leather, embroidered, with press-stud fastenings at the wrist. Right-hand glove marked 'Au Chevreau Royal L.Vaisière'. 1910-20. **£15-20/$25-33.**

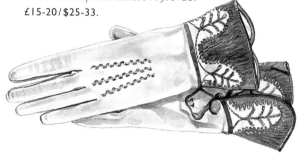

AN EXOTIC, STRONG BLACK NET, unlined evening coat, cut like a man's swallow-tail with scalloped edges. Machine embroidered in black chain-stitch with meandering pattern of stylized flowers – some with flossed silk highlights. It has elbow-length sleeves and fastens at the waist with press studs. Very elegant and feminine. Good condition. You could *easily* wear it now. 1912-14. **£25/$40.**

ANOTHER, SIMILAR JACKET – but this one more for boudoir wear. Very fussy and frilly, in cream crêpe de Chine and lots of lace. There is a long, floppy collar with bobbly fringing at the point where it fastens with two hooks and eyes. Machined and hand sewn. Fairly good condition – a few small holes. Very pretty-pretty. About 1912. **£30-40/$50-66.**

A SHIRT-BLOUSE OF black and white striped cotton, with separate white starched collar and linked cuffs. Drawn into centre back waist with tapes that tie in front. All machine sewn. Very governess/ senior typist looking. About 1910. **£20-30/ $33-50.**

PAIR OF FINE WHITE COTTON French knickers with wide legs, scalloped edges, white embroidered with button-flies. Elasticated waist and 22 inches in length. Label: 'Bel: Broid Lingerie. This Garment made of Tarantulle' (trade name for a lightweight cotton). About 1920. £35/$58.

THORN-PROOF TWEED 'sports' suit in shades of brown and cream with single-breasted, hip-length jacket (lining frail) that has patch pockets and high-buttoned (wind-proof) collar and lapels. Originally, there was a buttoned half-belt, now missing. The skirt is cut to above the ankle, with lined front panel and extra large, tough, inner pocket (for all the things country pursuiting ladies would need to tote around with them). This is a splendid, masculine-looking tailor-made, worn, patched, darned, but still admirable and, because such active clothes got worn out, rare. I've had 'Lady Gertrude' in the collection for ages and I still get a thrill every time I look at her. She must have been quite a girl. 1910-15. £80-95/$132-155.

HEAVY, BLACK WOOL CLOTH CAPE, with reverse of cloth a black/white tartan check. No armholes or hand slits. It has a small, flat collar and fastens with 4 large, plain buttons. At one time there was an attached hood, now missing. Not pretty, but well made. It was worn during the First World War and possibly up to the 1930s. It has survived moth, two wars and poor storage! Very wearable. £40-45/$66-75 if in good condition.

The sort of cape that every working-class girl and woman possessed. The style was already a hundred years old in 1900.

LONG (74 INCHES), fringed, spun silk 'muffler' in a pattern of muted colours (heather, green, yellow, black and dark blue). Really lovely: The Arbiter of Good Taste wants it. Good condition. About 1918. £25-35/$40-58 upwards.

PARASOL IN WHITE embroidered cotton with a graceful wooden stick and handle. Opens into a large, domed shape (to go over the big hats). Fair condition (small tears near the ferrule and handle and it has lost its decorative finial, which often happens). 1910. £20-30/$33-50. (See Plate 2.)

Many clothes became front fastening during these years – easier to manage sans lady's maid.

WHITE CAMBRIC (fine linen) blouse, shaped by tiny pin tucks, with small 'wing' collar and inserts of cotton lace. Frilled cuffs and front fastened by (hidden) small linen buttons and loops, but decorated with two large embroidered buttons. Professionally hand sewn. Ladylike, charming, wearable. Excellent condition. 1910-15. **£45-75 / $75-120**.

PLAIN BLACK, SATIN BAR-STRAP evening shoes with 2½-inch lacquered heels studded with *diamanté*. Inside shoe marked: 'Imported by S. Patara and Co, Battery Road, Singapore. Made in Paris'. Fair to good condition (but danced a lot...). **£30-45 / $50-75**. (*See Plates 3 and 7.*)

PAIR OF BLACK SATIN 'Tango' dance shoes. These are ribbon laced, ankle height, with Cuban heels and bow trimmed with *diamanté* at the front. Rather exotic and in good condition. 1914-20. **£45-50 / $75-82**. (*See also Plate 3.*)

GREY, CHECKED, LIGHT, crisp, silk day dress, trimmed black, with long, cuffed sleeves and mid-calf-length, flared skirt from a natural, sashed waist. The slightly 'bloused' bodice has a small peplum frill over the hips (it looks like a separate jacket) and is worked on a front-fastening inner bodice with long, black-edged revers – and over it an attached lace collar. Machine and hand sewn. Label (on stay strap): Madame Florence Clay, 117 Bridal Street, Birmingham. The dress, entirely original, is an example of the mid-First World War years, showing the 'military' 2-piece influence. As such it is uncommon. 1916-18. **£90-100 / $148-165**.

DRESS MADE FROM NATURAL, unbleached linen, the bodice a tabard over a net 'inner' with long linen sleeves. The skirt, with 3 hefty frills at the hem, is fairly full with high, loose waistline (lots of poppers and hooks), the whole dress decorated with coarse, embroidered drawn and 'pulled' thread work (like old-fashioned antimacassars). It sounds awful, doesn't it? But, though her hanger appeal is limited, when worn, she's a charmer! It was made for hot weather, for the bride of an Indian Army officer in 1913. Label on waistband. 'Fraulein Bertha Schwarz. Robes & Confections. Freiburg'. ('Confections' does not mean sweets, but off-the-peg clothes.) This dress has character, is unusual and in original order. £175-200/$300-330. (See Plate 3.)

EVENING PURSE (9 inches across) in amber velvet, professionally made with hand quilted pattern set on a gilt and enamel frame with chain handle. It is lined with silk. 1918-20. £35-40/$58-66.

BROWN, POLISHED LEATHER BAG (7 inches square), over-sewn at edges with embossed 'picture' inset in lighter shade. Inner compartments on metal frame, including coin purse; held by a single hand-strap secured by curly metal hooks. (Inside there is a little hinged rouge pot with the words 'Tattoo USA' embossed on its chased lid.) Nice condition. Handbags like this are very collectable. 1915-20. £35-50/$58-82 (especially with a period knick-knack inside!).

VERY LARGE (13 INCHES ACROSS) silver thread crochet evening bag worked in a robust 'bobbles' design (I think it may represent grapes), lined with grey silk and set on an ornate, pierced silver frame with tasselled, silver cord handle. Probably crafted at home. 1910-20. £65-85/$108-140.

Tassels are everywhere, taking the eye down to the hips, previewing the look that was to become fashionable in the 1920s.

A WHITE FUR BAG (7 × 6 inches) with embossed flowers on a polished metal frame with snap, and a 28-inch cord handle with beaded tassels. The bag is lined and has a tiny coin purse. I don't know what fur it is (I don't wish to know!) but on the front there is a small, decorative 'bear' mask, with open, toothy mouth, glass eyes and his claws tucked under his chin. Unusual; probably French. 1910-15. **£45/$75 upwards.**

A SPLENDID 'DOROTHY' BAG (12 × 9 inches), the basic material saffron-coloured satin, but overlaid with browny-fawn lace, decorated with wreaths of silk roses and stiff bronze braid. It 'pulls up' on long, bronze cord handles. Nicely homemade. (I've another one that has a looking-glass attached to the underside of the purse – a clever idea.) 1910-20. **£20/$33.**

Fascinatingly, the basic uncluttered style of this dress gives strong clues to the images that will prevail during the next two decades.

O NE OF THE MOST ELEGANT pieces in the entire collection. Plain black, silk satin evening dress in a straight but fluid, wrap-over form, cut with small train. Also, loosely attached, is a sleeveless waistcoat with long fronts and a long, narrow, square-ended train extending a couple of feet, made from a 'net' of wide mesh, black silk cord which is completely covered with large beads and medallions of French jet (black glass) and caught, half way up, with a large black velvet bow. Mainly hand sewn. It is an amazing piece! It works on a silk inner structure and has platoons of hooks and eyes and poppers to anchor it – but the effect is breathtakingly simple. I have always believed it to be by an important designer, but there is no label. Just ravishing design. I paid **£175/$300** for it in the early 1980s, but doubtless 'Solange', as I call her, would be worth more now (especially with an authenticated maker). 1914-20. (See Plate 3.)

MEN'S UNDERWEAR 1910-1920

P AIR OF WHITE, SLIGHTLY GAUZY, cotton combinations. With shallow 'boat' neck, no sleeves, fly-front buttoning, neck to crotch, while at the back there is a 'trap door' flap, fastened across back with one button. Label: 'Vassar Comfort to the Wearer'. Although men had worn woolly combinations from the late nineteenth century, this style of lightweight 'Unit Suit' was an American idea, introduced for summer wear after the First World War and increasingly popular across Europe during the 1920s. It's not exactly easy-peasy to get in and out of. Even so, I've not seen another like it, but you may be luckier! About 1920. £25-30/$40-66.

THE 1920S PINK KNEES AND JAZZ

Everybody, I'm certain, has a ready image of the 1920s as a fun time. These years conjure up the picture of young people happy to be released from the grim jaws of war and set on shocking the grown-ups with new ideas for living. There was a feeling of relief, a relaxation after terrible constraints, which certainly extended to the shape of the clothes during this period. Girls, shameless creatures, cut their hair, made-up their faces, wore skirts to their rosy-rouged knees, went to picture shows, danced like dervishes, smoked and were generally thought to be less ladylike than their mothers or grandmothers. As women moved further towards emancipation, fashionable lady journalists wrote that the ideal female figure was straight and boyish, the breasts 'undiscovered', the waist forgotten. I imagine men thought this form was far from pleasurable, their only consolation the hips, emphasized by the shortening skirts that revealed those modern legs. Mind you, not all men were gratified: the clergy declared short skirts the work of the devil, unpleasing in the eyes of the

Almighty. Which is quite ridiculous when you think how He invested in Adam and Eve.

By the end of the 1920s, a number of dramatic events had taken place: the General Strike in 1926; the first 'talking' movies were shown in Britain in 1928; and the Wall Street Crash in 1929, setting off an economic depression that reverberated worldwide. Artificial silk was on the market from 1921 (given the name Rayon in 1924), people listened to broadcasts on the wireless and there was an increasing number of motor cars. Wealthy holiday-makers could travel by aeroplane to warm foreign lands, especially since Coco Chanel had made a sun-tan acceptably enhancing to female charms. In essence, it was a time when more and more women, particularly from the working classes, came slightly more confidently into their own. The home dress-maker still flourished and there were lots of off-the-peg clothes, but if you were rich, superb *haute couture* still reigned supreme throughout the Western world.

CLOTHES OF THE 1920S

I've lugged down two huge cases of stuff and a big box of shoes and bags. It took me much longer than I thought it would because the rail with the dresses on had got very mixed up. I spent half an hour tidying up and restoring some semblance of order, and I think I've done pretty well in finding good examples. I did want to get out the real 1920s characters from the collection to give you an idea of the period's exhilarating novelty and joy.

> Since finishing the last section and re-starting, I've had the 'flu and experienced a burst water tank. Water deluged through three floors in as many minutes (fortunately missing the Costume Room, apart from a box of hat feathers) and the vicar, poor man, nearly lost his voice during the Christmas Services. And, oh dear, funerals are piling up because of the exceptionally cold weather. However, enough of domestic gloom – let's continue with the scintillating 1920s...

IF THE 1920S IS FAMOUS for one garment, it is surely the bead dress. Red cotton gauze, sleeveless dance dress covered with silver (bugle) beads; the low waist defined with a floral design, repeated at the neck. The skirt has a 'Van Dycked' hem (up and down points), typical around 1924. Excellent condition. **£200-300/$330-500.** (*See Plate 4.*)

One of the most persistent decorative influences from 1922 onwards was Ancient Egypt: the discovery of Tutankhamun's tomb inspired a thousand designs.

ANOTHER DRESS, MADE from black chiffon with cap sleeves, the whole worked in vertical stripes of black beads with neck and skirt decorated with coloured beads in a vibrant floral pattern. I like this dress because the design is classic, uncluttered and very smart; it would grace a party even now. Very good condition (often the beads are missing or loose). 1924-26. **£150-250/$248-412.**

A FINE, BLACK COTTON NET TABARD (just a hole for the neck) covered in tiny jet beads and black sequins (*paillettes*) in a swirly design. Such an enchanting thing, worn over either a black or coloured base dress, turns a plain frock into an exciting after-dark ensemble. Simple, clever and very French: the best beaded and sequinned clothes were made in France. **£100-150/$165-248.**

BEAD DRESSES

About ten years ago, an original 1920s bead dress might have cost more than two or three hundred pounds, but with the arrival of 'modern' bead-worked dresses imported from India, 'real' bead dresses took a knock. So, unless the piece has a sought-after label or it is staggeringly lovely, the market price for genuine 1920s beaded garments is not huge. It may still increase, as their quality of design and colour is usually superior to that of the late twentieth-century versions.

Because of the weight of beads, these dresses always need to be carefully stored. I lie mine flat on pieces of sheeting and loosely 'Swiss roll' them and store them in a box.

A LUSTROUS GOLD, RED, BLUE and orange metallic brocade knee-length, wrap-over evening coat, the cuffs and hem faced with deep borders of rust-coloured velvet. Lined with blue silk and with a frivolous, bright blue ostrich feather collar. About 1925. **£285/$470**. *(See Plate 4.)*

C REAM WOOL SERGE SUIT with three-quarter length, lined jacket with narrow revers, flat-pleated from the 'easy' waist with a centre tab, about 7 inches, which fastens the 3 pearl buttons. The skirt is to mid-calf, also pleated, with hooks and eyes and 'poppers' to fasten at the side. Chanel-influenced, impeccably tailored, the style timeless from 1916 and constantly revived, even now. Label: 'Madame Lille, Robes and Mantles, 24 Southbourne Grove, Bournemouth'. A smart little number for strolling through the Winter Gardens in about 1920. 2-piece, tailor-mades are not plentiful from this period. **£80-100/$132-165**. *(See Plate 4.)*

A STUNNING, ELEGANT BELT BUCKLE, 4½ inches long, made from square-cut *(baguette)* pastes set in silvered metal, with two eliptical centre-pieces of blue 'marbled' Bakelite. Marked: 'Made in France'. The sort of thing that would have been seen at the Paris *Exposition des Arts Décoratifs et Industriels Modernes* of that year. About 1925. **£45/$75**.

Now, there are lots of lovely buckles, buttons and costume pieces to find — reasonably priced, excellently designed, non-precious 'jewels' from the 1920s. It's a matter of getting your eye in.

These simple styles were lovingly made to wear with the veils held in place with bands of orange blossom placed low across the eyebrows (very Mary Pickford).

A MID-CALF WEDDING DRESS, the shapeless look – nicely homemade, the bodice and sleeves cut in one from soft silk satin. Low waistline, emphasized with a yoke of satin flower rosettes with beaded centres. The skirt is overlaid with a layer of shiny 'parlour-window' curtain lace. No fastenings, it just slips on over the head. It sounds awful, but it looks sweet when worn. Mine is in good condition (this is so important) and is typical of thousands of wedding dresses from 1919 to 1923. They now cost anything between £50/ $82 and £150/$248 depending on whether they are home or professionally made, how decorative they are and, vitally, their condition. 1921. (*See Plate 4.*)

A SILVER 'HELMET' BRIDAL HEAD-DRESS made of metal thread with 'earphones' decorated with wax orange blossom, also arranged round the brow. 1923. £30-50/ $50-82. Net veil with flower motifs. About 1920. £50-60/ $82-100. (*See Plate 4.*)

A N ORCHID PINK NIGHTDRESS made from silk chiffon, the bodice gathered onto a simple band of lace under the bust and threaded with baby blue ribbon; the shoulder straps and split-front hem also trimmed with lace. Very pretty, nice condition. About 1920. £50/$82 upwards.

A PADDED, BLACK SATIN nightdress case (17 × 9 inches) in a 'roll' shape, lined with rose pink silk, decorated with bronze braid, tassels and swag of pink silk flowers and 'bobbles' on the front flap. Professionally made in the

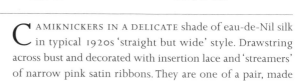

'Arabian' style and, doubtless, meant to look like a cushion on the bed. Good condition (some girl got it as a present and never used because it was easier to shove the nightie under the pillow). £25- 35/$40-58.

C AMIKNICKERS IN A DELICATE shade of eau-de-Nil silk in typical 1920s 'straight but wide' style. Drawstring across bust and decorated with insertion lace and 'streamers' of narrow pink satin ribbons. They are one of a pair, made as part of a wedding trousseau in about 1924. Fair to good condition (a couple of darned holes – they were obviously much loved!). **£30/$50 for the pair.**

PAIR OF OPAQUE, PINKY-CREAM silk stockings with fine arrow clocks at the ankles. They are lovely, and look as though they have never been worn. There is no way of telling which hosiery company they came from, but they may have been part of a wedding trousseau. About 1920. **£15/$25.**

PAIR OF PALE, ONE-INCH WIDE, blue satin ribbon garters backed by (slack) elastic. There is a little rosette decoration on each. They did belong to a bride in 1922. Limp and faded, but interesting. **£80/$132.** I've another pair, peachy pink, unworn, still in their gift box (they made cheeky presents). **£28/$46.**

BRASSIÈRE - CALLED 'a bandeau brassière' – made from coarse 'Lever's' lace, 42 inches along with tie tapes at each end (they crossed behind and tied under the bust). Depth at widest point (front) 8 inches, with two tiny cased 'bones'. Cream ribbon shoulder straps and 'stay' hook on tape at centre front. Marked: 'Venus [there were a lot of these goddesses about] Brassière. Model 381 Size 44'. Good condition. About 1920. **£25/$40 upwards (especially if it has a manufacturer's mark).**

BRAS

You may need to go to sales or specialist dealers to find 1920s brassières. They are scarce, but these bras are amusing because the idea of a 'flattener' (the flattened frontage was all the rage) is decidedly *not* in fashion at the moment of writing, although I dare say it will be again one day.

WHITE COTTON GAUZE, long-sleeved, cuffed blouse with deep pointed collar, white embroidered with drawn thread-work; the revers continue in a soft roll to the tape tie waist. No other fastenings. It looks summery and unstructured – not tight and 'upright' like the 1900s examples. It is still very wearable. Professionally sewn in 1920-25. **£35/$58** upwards.

Early twentieth-century day clothes are less available than evening wear. It's the old story: day clothes wore out and were scrapped but evening clothes had less wear and were often saved for sentimental reasons.

THE SEE-ME-THROUGHNESS of the above blouse would have been compensated for by wearing a full slip such as this oyster-coloured silk short slip in a 'straight' style with a scallop-edged hem. The shoulder straps are made of the same material and the 'v' is cut-work, embroidered in fawn silks. Entirely hand sewn. About 1920. **£15-20/$25-33**.

ALONG-SLEEVED, SUMMER day dress made from a fine silk/cotton gauze with blue ground and abstract design in black, grey and coral, the hem sash and vestee front made of fine black silk. The understated, low-waisted dress was made from a length of Liberty material bought in the shop's sale of 1928. Simple and charming. **£35/$58**.

PAIR OF DAY-WEAR snakeskin shoes with bar-strap and chunky Louis heels. Marked inside: 'Harrods, Ltd'. Very smart! **£35-50/$58-82**. (*See also Plate 4*.)

PAIR OF FINE SILVER leather evening shoes with almond-shaped toes, 2-inch Louis heels and buttoned bar-straps. Extremely wearable. 1925. **£30-40/$50-66**.

SHOES

The snakeskins shown opposite are typical of the look of 1920s shoes. You'll be able to find a number of these shoes in wearable sizes – not everybody had the doll feet evidenced by so many Victorian and Edwardian shoes. This could be a fascinating area in which to collect. Look for interesting materials and for makers' labels. The better the make and condition, the more you will have to pay.

Stockings, as they came into view with the shortened skirts, became classed as accessories rather than underwear. They can be found in good condition, since they were usually well looked after, darned, pressed and stored, often in special 'stocking cases' and sachets. Pair of peach pink (supposedly flesh-coloured) artificial silk stockings with clocks, neatly darned. 1925-30. **£2/$3 upwards.**

A PAIR OF GREY ARTIFICIAL silk stockings. Unworn, with maker's label, 'Iris Brand', still attached. The stockings stamped at welt and foot: 'Superior Quality. Wear-resisting and durable. English make. Non-ladder. Double Sole and High Spliced Ankles'. (Since Elizabethan times there were problems in making a nice fit about the ankles.) About 1920. **£10-12/$17-20.**

Although the new invention of Rayon revolutionized stocking manufacture, real silk stockings were still kept for best.

STOCKING BOXES

Just for fun, it is a lovely idea to keep a watch out for the boxes stockings were packed in. From the 1920s to the 1950s, these were often attractively designed with charming decorations and evocative pictures on the lids. Morley, Ballito, Seal Brand – all the big hosiery manufacturers did them. They can cost as little as a pound, depending on condition, and how attractive they are!

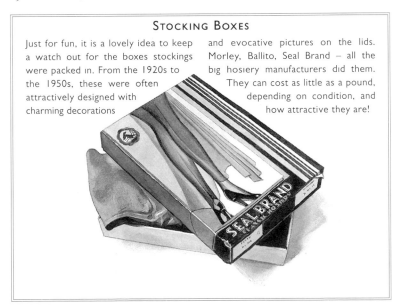

A DEEP CLOCHE HAT – the sort everyone associates with the 1920s – in a striking, rich blue velvet with tiny one-inch curved brim decorated with a large, flat, pink velvet flower in the centre, with smaller petals, like wings, at the side. Lined in black silk. No label but professionally made. Very good condition. 1920-25. **£65-75/$108-123.** (*See Plate 4.*)

A CHARMING PAIR OF short gloves in biscuit-coloured doe skin with embroidered spines and deep gold leather, buttoned cuffs, embroidered with colourful flowers. There is a tiny oriental doll hanging from the left cuff. Superbly hand sewn. Stamped inside: 'Grands Magasins du Louvre'. Good condition. About 1920. **£12-15/$20-25.**

V ERY LONG (24 INCHES) white doe skin evening gloves with 4-button wrist closure. Fine quality (just the thing for dinner at the Ritz – and, no, they didn't eat a meal with their gloves on, but took them off completely). Stamped inside right glove: 'Made Specially For – A. Bide – 158a, New Bond Street. Size 6'. Stamped in left glove: 'Made in France'. 1920-30. **About £10/$17.**

A N AMAZING CIGARETTE HOLDER made of silvered metal in an enamel outer case, with amber end-pieces. It measures 10 inches when closed, extending, like a telescope, to a staggering 41 inches when fully open. My mother told me that holders like this were novelties in the late 1920s and early 1930s, the idea being that you could smoke near an open window, thereby pointing the smoke outside rather than into your partner's face or the drawing-room. A very good idea. Attractive holders sell from a few pounds to incredible sums if they are decorative or made of precious materials. This one is certainly unusual. **£40-60/$66-100.**

> I am decidedly against smoking (the vicar even more so, since he suffers with dreadful sinusitis) but, at one time, it was innocently regarded as a sophisticated social accomplishment. Smoking accessories became part of a woman's dress.

P LUMP, WHITE OSTRICH FEATHER BOA, 6 feet long. In good condition. A fashion decidedly featuring feathers (boas, large fans, shoulder capes, collars and bed-jackets) came in during the 1920s, providing lightweight cover for the skimpy evening dresses of the period. Feathers also looked, and felt, sensual. 1920-25. **£25-30 / $40-50.**

MESH PURSES

Mesh evening purses were popular from the early twentieth century and were particularly in vogue to complement the fluid styles of the 1920s. They were made in Germany, France, England and America. Really superb, beautifully enamelled examples can be priced into hundreds of pounds. Bags and purses from this period are made in literally hundreds of different styles, in all sorts of materials and with a range of interesting frames or closures. Upstairs I have a box of fabric bags (some sewn at home) which have fascinating imitation ivory, tortoiseshell, amber or carved frames (the best ones from France and Germany) all manufactured from composition materials. They are worth between £10 / $17 and £45 / $75, depending on condition and design.

S MALL FRAME EVENING PURSE (5 × 6 inches) with blue glass 'snap' and chain handle made of baby-fine gold and silver metallic mesh in a lattice pattern, with fringe of mesh 'lace' decorating the bottom. Lined with silk. Good condition. No maker's mark. About 1920. **£35-40 / $58-66.**

N O SELF-RESPECTING FLAPPER could be without her long beads, could she? They're part of the kit. I have several ropes, but this one I know bopped throughout the 1920s. It is made of heavy, pink, marbled glass beads, with strong gilt metal links. **£30-40 / $50-66.**

D ULL METAL, ROUND POWDER compact with small looking-glass – 2 inches across – embossed with grotesque mask (I think this was a joke!). Stamped on the back: 'Vinolia *Aralys* compact' with patent number. 1920-30. **£6-8 / $10-13.**

POWDER COMPACTS

A wonderful field for collectors is powder compacts. You can find compacts in antique shops, fairs, flea markets, car boot sales or, maybe, cajole them from elderly aunts! The smaller the compact the earlier it is going to be. I find compacts intriguing because they are often imaginatively designed and are intensely feminine. Women tell (or think) a lot of secrets to their reflections.

SMALL, GILT METAL POWDER compact enamelled with black and set with raised gilt flowers and coloured pastes. Interior good. 1925-30. **£10-15/$17-25**.

TINY BRASS (1½ INCHES) and green enamelled rouge pot – like a patch box – with lid containing looking-glass. Inside there is a petite lamb's wool puff with ivory handle. Charming and in good condition. **£15/$25 upwards**.

Between the Wars, swimming costumes and seaside stuff are fairly uncommon, as so much of it was worn to a frazzle and then got thrown away.

A WOMAN'S TWO-PIECE bathing-suit in black wool jersey, the long vest top with strap sleeves and deep 'v' back and front edged with black and orange stripes, repeated on the legs of the trunks. These have a tie-tape waist with a smart woven belt in shades of black and orange. No label, but simple, elegant, cheekily uni-sex, and, I suspect, French (Coco Chanel designed things just like this in the 1920s). Condition good (a bit of fade – a common state for early swimwear, of course), but unusual. **£50-60/$82-100**.

AN EXTRAORDINARY all-in-one bra and suspenders made in shiny pink cotton-backed satin and ecru textile lace. It fastens with hooks at the side and has two front suspenders hanging from frilly pink elastic webbing. The metal 'clips' have piggy pink composition buttons in a heart shape. Manufacturer: 'Twilfit'. Stamped inside: 'Discontinued Make. Not Guaranteed. Size 42'. Good condition (hardly worn – perhaps it was uncomfortable). 1925-30. **£10-12/$17-20**.

A SPIFFING HAT. A snug green and black jersey cap with pull-around 'scarf' pieces that clip together. Unworn and in original box marked: 'Turban-Lady Mad Cap. The Hat that Has Taken Fashion By Storm. Motoring/Walking/Skating/Shopping/Golfing. To Fit Everybody. Made by "Oceans of Notions" 3 shillings and 11 pence.' **£38/$62**.

Large wooden hat box with carrying strap and the owners initials painted on the side. About 1920. **£35/ $58.** (*See Plate 4.*)

Close-fitting 'helmet' hat made of blue felt with elastic chin-strap and buckle. About 1927. **£30/$50.** (*See Plate 5.*)

Men's underwear 1920

This time a large but superb pair of trunks, 42-inch waist and 26-inch leg length, in excellent condition. Made on a fitted linen yoke, with big, mother-of-pearl fly buttons, sturdily reinforced crutch and double loops for braces. The main fabric is an interesting 'perforated' woven cotton material which, the red woven label states, is 'Deimelin. Weight H of Dr. Deimel Underwear'. It's obviously an alternative to Aertex and was probably most comfortable to wear and easy to launder. I can imagine Dr Deimel with a matching vest, grey knitted knee socks and smoking a pipe – indeed all the advertisements that you see for men's underwear during the first half of this century tend towards this hearty, pipe-smoking image. The 'nothing sissy about me' look. 1920-25. **£15/$25.**

THE 1930S GLAMOROUS NIGHTS

I have a rather special regard for the 1930s. They seem to have been in my mind's eye all my conscious life, probably because the decade was my parents' hey-day and my childhood home was characterized by the 'new' style furnishings which they had bought in the early years of their marriage. The china – bright with gaudy, zig-zag patterns; the dining-room furniture – smooth, rounded and light-coloured (so different from the dark brown of my grandmother's home); the beds – glimmering with satiny counterpanes, topped with plump quilts, the down feathers trapped and pocketed by intricate machine embroidery on the top. People's homes – and their clothes – reflected a striving for a different life from that of their Victorian parents and were certainly heavily influenced by the escapism depicted in Hollywood films. It was a strange, wonderful, inspiring decade that by re-appraising the recent past provided glamour and brave, artistic expression. Sadly, it also brought frightening poverty and lack of jobs. In the end, the tragedy was that it heralded another war.

And fashion? Well, occasionally The Arbiter and I get the old family photographs out and while she exclaims and is amused by what I wore in the 1950s, she finds her grandmother's clothes of the 1930s 'brilliant' and wishes there was stuff like that now. The technical advantages for clothes in the 1930s were profound. The garment industry was supplying plenty of good quality manufactured clothes, and also *haute couture*. Abundant, small 'Madame' establishments in towns catered for middle-class women who now, possibly, had a 'little job' as well as running a home – meaning that they had a bit more money to spend on themselves. Plenty of fashion articles and advice appeared in magazines, and for the home dress-maker it was an exciting time. She could purchase very good paper patterns and choose from the cheaper new Rayon materials; and with the domestic work-horse, a sewing-machine, whizzing away in the front room, create a Paris model in one afternoon.

Totally biased.

There are many amusing 1930s facts and figures. Berlei (UK) brought in the first commercial system of sizing for women's bosoms: proper measurements and A/B/C cup fittings. 'D' came later, and goodness knows what letter they are up to now. In 1931, a national newspaper stated that 1500 lipsticks were being bought for every one sold previously – which is nice to know, since I approve of lipstick.

CLOTHES OF THE 1930S

The Arbiter of Good Taste thinks the 1930s is a most glamorous decade. She enjoys the whole slinky, Odeonesque style of it, which appears terribly smart and sophisticated. Certainly, there are some beautiful evening things, but I've tried to gather up a wide range of top clothes, undies, accessories and all sorts of bits and bobs to give you an overview of these ten years.

I do implore you to think not only about clothes, but also about all the bits and pieces of ephemera that surround the fashion industry and women's dress. You can have a collection of 'something to do with fashion' that costs very little and is still fascinating and informative. For example, I mentioned paper patterns: 'ordinary' dress patterns get turfed out, yet thirty years on, they become very collectable.

To START WITH, an amusing coat showing the indecisive mood that fashion displayed at the end of the 1920s and beginning of the 1930s. The hem lines wavered, not knowing whether to stay up or go down; some did both, and this 'dressy' coat is an example. Satin lined, made in a dropped-waist style with flared skirt that, while knee length in front, curves to a deep dip at the back. The 6-inch stiffened collar is designed to pull close around the head and pointed cuffs 'stand' in a similar way. The fabric is curious and a joy: heavy, stone-coloured silky brocade (like curtaining material) splashed with hot colours (lots of indigo, pink and orange) reminscent of Clarice Cliff ceramics, in a design that, on close examination, isn't the abstract you first thought but large, rather oriental vases of flowers. The material has been *purposely* reversed for making this outrageous coat! Machine and professionally hand sewn. No label. Some repair to lining. About 1930. **£60/$100 upwards.** (*See Plate 5.*)

Possibly this fabric is designed by a brilliant artist, Sonia Delaunay, 1885-1979, who was working as a textile designer in Paris from 1925. Her ideas were avant garde, but magic for those who dared to wear them.

A SLENDER, PURE SILK afternoon dress, with long dolman (cut in one with the bodice, deeper than magyar) sleeves, made in a bold, abstact zig-zag pattern of red, cream and navy. Lined throughout, the dress has a straight cut skirt to mid-calf and the bodice, with a 10-inch front opening, fastens with poppers — with 4 large cream buttons 'decorating' the outside, a device that is repeated on the right-hand side of the skirt. There is a separate self-sash slotted through loops at the waist. Label: 'Marshall & Snelgrove, Vere Street and Oxford Street, London. WI: Tea Gown Dept'. The condition of this dress is frail, the silk disintegrating in certain places (I suspect it was much worn in a hot climate), but it is a charming, ladylike gown of the sort that famous London and provincial department stores of the 1920s and 1930s must have made, bespoke, by the score, for middle- and upper-class ladies. The material is superb: textile designs become increasingly eye-catching and witty during the 1930s. 1930-34. About **£50-70/$82-115, but lots more if it could be established as Delaunay material**. *(See Plate 5.)*

PAIR OF WHITE BUCKSKIN and brown *glacé* kid (smooth, highly-polished leather), two-tone 'co-respondent' shoes with bar-strap and Cuban heels. Co-respondent shoes came in after the First World War – for men first – imitating the jaunty look flaunted on the Riviera by playboys. That's where Coco Chanel first realized the idea as a witty fashion for women's shoes, too. No label. Good condition. Size 6. About 1930. **£25-35/$40-58**. *(See Plate 4.)*

ANOTHER PAIR OF BROWN and white co-respondent shoes with slightly higher, slimmer heels than 1920s models and elegant 'acorn' tasselled lace ties across upper. Gold stamped inside: 'W.H. Smith & Hook Knowles, Ltd. 66 New Bond Street, London W1'. Also, inked code number of the client at the heel. These are beautifully made, classic shoes that you could easily wear now. 1936-38. **£35/$58**.

ANOTHER PAIR OF SHOES, for evening wear, made from Art Deco design of grey silk patterned in metallic thread with gold kid T-bar and *diamanté* buckle and 2-inch heels. Satin lined and in good condition. No label. 1930-35. **£35-40/$58-66**. *(See also Plate 5.)*

FLAT, RATHER SCULPTED sandals made of coral red calf with cream trim. Label: 'Brevitt Bouncers'. Good condition. About 1935. **£20/$33.** (*See Plate 5.*)

AWHISP OF AN EVENING DRESS – you can pull it through a wedding ring – made of the finest silk chiffon, floral patterned in orange, yellow and cream. Cut on the bias, the ankle-length skirt billows out from a tight bodice with little frilled sleeves and a modest neckline. Entirely hand sewn, model dress. No label. About 1930. **£30-40/$50-66.**

Elsa Schiaparelli made 'bows' high fashion in the 1930s.

LARGE DECORATIVE BOW (5 × 6 inches) appliqué, made from *diamanté* 'brilliants' and silver beads backed with stiff silk. Good design and condition. The sort of thing that would have been sewn onto an evening dress. It's pretty, and

there are other beaded bits like this to be found from a few pounds upwards. I smile when I get this out, because it was given to me, carefully wrapped, as it had always been, in a small paper bag of the 1930s advertising 'Radiance Toffee', Doncaster. I find quirky things like that endearing. About 1935. **£15-20/$25-33.**

SMALL, BROWN MOROCCO leather case (4 × 3 inches) containing mother-of-pearl sewing implements (including penknife) and separate section for needles. Embossed inside: 'Kirby, Beard & Co Ltd'. This established English firm originally made fitted luggage, travel bags and ladies' handbags but are probably best known in the late twentieth century for the famous 'Kirby' hair-grip. Poor condition, the things a tad rusty. About 1930. **£5/$8.**

HERE I MUST PUT IN my favourite dressing-case. It is 20 by 13 inches and 5 inches deep. Made of black Morocco leather with two plain silver metal clasps and a strong, covered handle. It is very severe and serviceable looking on the outside, but, on opening, stylish it is, with a big 's'! Lined with pale, oyster pink Ottoman silk (that heavily ribbed stuff), with each compartment edged in black leather. It has most of its original fittings, and what is so smart is the way that all the glass pots and brushes have their lids and backs done in black enamel, decorated with tiny circles of marquisites. There's lots of room for your nightie, etc., and, sensibly, it has a large oval looking-glass slotted into the case lid, secured by a swivel. Of course it's French. No label – but you just know it's from Paris. Overall it's in 'nicely worn' condition. **£120/$200 upwards.** (*See Plate 5.*)

A 1930S NOVELTY. A pink, satined, 5-inch, sole-shaped lamb's wool puff is fixed onto an elegant long handle. Tucked into the ribbon decoration is a little verse: 'When Evening Gown you wish to don/And other means you lack/Just put some powder on my wool/And gently pat your back'. I love it! **£10/$17.**

T HIS WAS STILL A DECADE in which to dress up the servants for the amusement of visitors. Along with the fish-knives and doilies, you could have the maid serve tea wearing 'fancy' over her trim plain dress. I have a set (cap, apron, collar and cuffs) made in pale pink organdie, embroidered in scallops of fawn (I expect her dress was fawn), the cap having slots for the headband. **£25/$40.**

P AIR OF HEAVY-WEIGHT, steel hair-curling tongs with wooden handles. Well used. From the 1930s, curls were fashionable. Even now I can recall the smell of singeing hair as my mother set to and made me, a straight-haired wench, ready for parties in the 1940s. It was quite an art, involving heating the tongs in the fire, wiping them with a rag and then winding the damp hair into a smooth sausage on the steel, clamping its jaws tight for a few seconds and then releasing the warm curl against your head. About 1930. Curling tongs, memories and a hairdo can be yours for less than **£10/$17.**

THE ULTIMATE HAIR NET

Perhaps tennis is your game? If so, you'd certainly want this. I quote from two sides of the packet: 'The "Portia" Registered, Washable and Hygienic Non-Flam Tennis Cap-Net. The Perfect Shade for Lady Tennis Players. Fits Everybody. Keeps the Hair Perfectly Tidy. Entirely Free From Danger. Optically Perfect. Easily the Best Tennis Shade for Woman Players yet Invented. It Has No Equal. BEWARE OF IMITATIONS'. And that's all before you've even opened the flap. Wow! Actually, after that build up, it's disappointing – a cream and green curved eye-shade sewn onto a heavy-gauge hair-net cum snood. But it was doubtless a giant step forward for Wimbledon lasses with Bad Hair Days in the 1930s (and they got shorts to play in as well by 1934).

O R YOU CAN WEAR YOUR 'Jo'sella Supreme Angora Sports Hat, Suitable for All Wear and Can be Worn Comfortably in Many Ways'. This information is printed on the lid of the (9 × 3 inches) box, and inside is the rolled, green felt hat – pudding shaped and a bit moth-eaten, but nonetheless an example of the 'get out and slay 'em' headgear favoured by lady golfers in the 1930s. **£10-12/$17-20.**

To complete this outfit, there is a matching, peaked cap with ear-pieces and chin-strap, a huge pair of leather mittens and a pair of woolly socks. Effectively, you'd look like a skiing postman.

A SKI OUTFIT. TAILORED, 2-piece jacket and trousers made from dark navy blue gaberdine (it reminds me of my old school raincoat). The jacket, double-breasted with high buttoned collar, buttoned cuffs, patch pockets and belt, is lined with dark red twilled silk. The trousers are long, baggy, with pockets, strong waist strap, under-foot elastic and robust tie-tapes at the ankles. Label: 'H.A. Beal, Regent Street, London. w.1.' (possibly 'made to measure'). Very good condition. 1930. **£150-180/$248-300,** as all sports' stuff is fairly unusual.

A LONG, BIAS-CUT SCARF of artificial silk crêpe in a black and white Art Deco design. Real smart! Here's another uncomplicated yet abundant area for a new collector to explore. The 1920s and 1930s produced some beautiful scarves, and so did every decade thereafter. They sell from from a few pounds upwards, depending on condition, design, designer, rarity of design. **£10-12/$17-20**. (*See Plate 4.*)

L ARGE STRAW SUN-HAT with deep shading brim, trimmed with red, white and blue silk scarf. Label: 'Fortnum and Mason'. About 1935. **£40/$66**. (*See Plates 5 and 14.*)

G REY WOOLLEN FABRIC gloves with gauntlet cuffs, which are decorated at the tip with large self-button and button-hole. Label: 'Yvonne and Agnew'. One glove mothed. About 1935. **50p/80 cents**.

I've found some typical examples of 1930s gloves, when wide cuffs were in fashion.

P AIR OF PALE FAWN kid gloves with flared cuffs decorated with punch-work. Beautifully made; the maker's mark is blurred. **£6/$10**.

P AIR OF GREY, FINE COTTON JERSEY gloves with wide, petalled cuffs, trimmed with white stitching. Stamped inside: 'Made in Germany'. **£4-5/$6-8**.

D ECORATED GLOVE BOX MARKED 'Marshall & Snelgove', containing pair of long, white kid evening gloves with 3-button wrist, stamped: 'Penberthy. Court Glove Maker, Duke Street and Oxford Street'. **£10-12/$17-20**.

P AIR OF SHORT, WHITE KID trimmed with black embroidery gloves with flared cuffs, stamped inside: 'Made in Czechoslovakia'. **£12-15/$20-25**.

HANDKERCHIEFS

Look out for fashion handkerchiefs, dating from 1920s to the 1950s. Many ladies favoured a pretty, artful hanky tucked here, there or anywhere as an up-beat accessory. A whole range of lovely not-to-blow-your-nose-on handkerchiefs can be found: designed with anything from spots, cubes and abstracts to animals, florals and film-stars. Liberty & Co. designed stunners. **£1-10/$1.65-17 upwards, according to quality and design.**

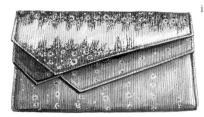

ENVELOPE HANDBAG (11 × 9 inches) made from imitation reptile skin with double button-down flap and lined interior, plus small coin purse. The imitation leather used here is a sort of Rexine. There is a wrist strap at the back. **£10-12/$17-20**.

A NAVY LEATHER (11 × 5 INCHES) clutch handbag, with chromed frame and large 'snaps'. This shape sometimes called 'steamer' because it looked vaguely like an ocean liner. The bag has a silk-lined interior with fixed coin purse – lined dark one side (for copper) and white the other (for silver) and pocket for glass. Label: 'British Made'. Good condition. A popular style throughout the 1930s. **£12-15/$20-25**.

A NOTHER FLAT, OBLONG BAG in ruby suede (10 × 7 inches) with press-stud on flap front. Interior lined with red watered silk, containing zipped compartment, fixed, kid-lined coin purse and a section for lipstick and looking-glass. Fresh, clean condition. Classic design. **£30-35/$50-58**.

S TEAMER-SHAPED, brown, fine-pleated silk purse with chrome and faux amber frame. Lined with brown watered silk, containing fixed coin purse with the usual division for copper and silver. Afternoon into evening purse in fairly good condition. 1930s. **£10/$17**.

A GORGEOUS BLUE SILK evening bag (6 × 7 inches) with chased, 'real' (sterling) silver frame overlaid with black enamel, set with marcasite decoration in an Art Deco style. Silk-lined interior and silver twist-link handle. No maker's name, but exquisite in every detail. An acceptable, usable present, even now. **£150-180/$248-300**.

SMALL, SQUARE POWDER COMPACT with foiled-back, Perspex lid, illustrating a kingfisher. It has a polished metal looking-glass and maker's name inside: 'Tap-Flap. Gwenda. Regd.' £10/$17.

Compacts were often given as presents and never used.

SHAPED LIKE A TINY, flat unopened Kodak camera of the 1930s, this true 'compact' contains sections for powder, lipstick and, inevitably during the 1930s, cigarettes. It is a droll accessory, possibly made in Germany. It is 3 × 2 inches, made from gilt metal and dark red patterned celluloid resembling tortoiseshell. Good condition. £30/$50.

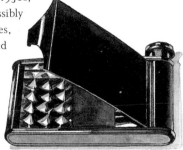

ANOTHER SMALL, SQUARE COMPACT in silver metal, engraved with an Art Deco design, with looking-glass and powder puff. Maker's name inside: 'Boots'. Slight wear, looking-glass cracked. £6-7/$10-12.

CREAM ENAMELLED, GOLD-PLATED, oblong 'vanity case' (4 × 2 inches), very heavy to hold on its flexi-metal handle (you could ward off unwanted attentions with this!), with tiny 'gemstone' and marcasite decoration. A double catch allows each side of case independent opening and contains sections to hold powder, rouge, lipstick, comb, cigarettes, holder, matches and postage stamps. Engraved 'Park Lane' on catch. Doubling as an evening purse, this was known as a 'Super Flap-Jack'. Good condition. 1937. £35-40/$58-66.

ELEGANT, SQUARE (2 × 2 inches) chrome and black enamel compact, initialled 'M' in marcasite with Art Deco design on lid. Still with original felt cover. Some interior damage. About 1935. £12-15/$20-25.

SMALL, DECORATIVE DRESS CLIP (usually made in pairs, these became increasingly popular during the 1930s) made from silvered metal, set with faux bloodstone, brilliants and enamelled motif. About 1933. £2-3/$3-5.

Everyone had knitted bathers (even though they were wretched to wear, sagged embarrassingly when wet and stank like a wet dog as they dried).

Black, heavy wool, home-knitted bathing 'dress' (because it still has an all-in-one skirt over the trunks) decorated with bands of orange wool. In very good condition. Since holidays and 'going swimming' were rare occurences in ordinary homes, this homemade style dominated throughout the 1920s and 1930s for working-class women (and became only for kids by the 1940s/50s). The point is, what happened to them? You're absolutely right. They went 'thick', got mothed... and were binned. I'd given up hope of ever finding one when I was given this. **£15-30/$25-30? But priceless to an ardent collector!**

Now, this next swimsuit is a manufactured example: a machine jersey-knit, one-piece, skirted costume patterned in 2-inch red and cream toadstools on a navy background, with navy 'underneaths'. It has long, jersey straps (one cream, one red) that cross at the back, slip through a Bakelite loop and then tie in the front. I haven't seen another from this time with such an amusing motif – poisonous toadstools would be quite daring amongst all the sombre black knits. Apart from neat darns at the crutch, it's in good condition. About 1935. **£20-30/$33-50.**

SWIMMING CAPS

To complete the bathing-beauty look, a green marble-effect rubber bathing helmet, with moulded sections for the ears! Rubber chin strap perished. And a pair of red rubber beach shoes with cream trims – much worn, now also perishing fast. I realize these don't sound fetching, but both items are interesting and rare. They'd be worth only a couple of pounds and yet, to someone who knows, they're wonderful things.

While on the subject of beachwear, don't forget the oriental beach kimonos and the paper sunshades that went with them – from Monte Carlo to Margate.

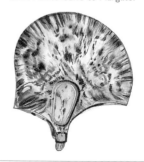

A 'v'-neck afternoon dress of black silk with bright floral pattern in red, yellow and turquoise, cut on the bias, with long sleeves that have a cape of frills at the shoulder. There is a self-sash and insertions (godets) to give fullness at the hem. Fastened with press-studs on the side seam. Beautifully made (machined and hand finished). No label. Very sculptured (you'd need a slip underneath). I bet she felt 'Jean Harlow' when she did the shopping in this. Good condition. £40-50/$66-82.

A SIDE-SADDLE RIDING HABIT in navy cavalry twill, the hip-length jacket in 2-button, cutaway style (like a man's evening tail-suit) with two pockets and hacking vents at the back. The boot-length skirt is an apron or 'safety' skirt: it fully covers the front of the body and then wraps round the back in a short, side-buttoning flap. Under this she would have worn riding breeches, probably made from white twill or doe skin. Label: 'Busvine. By Special Appointment to Her Late Majesty The Queen'. Tailor's label noting customer: 'Busvine Ltd. 4 Brook Street, London. (Typed) 4/2/35. Miss Palmer'. Still in good condition. 1935. £150/$248 upwards.

Busvine was founded in 1863 and closed in 1939. They made bespoke riding habits for Queen Alexandra and created the first side-saddle outfit for her. They were patronised by all the best people, including Queen Mary.

BY SPECIAL APPOINTMENT To HER LATE MAJESTY THE QUEEN BUSVINE LIMITED LONDON. 4 BROOK ST.W

BY THE EARLY 1930S, hats were either chirpy, sleek to the head felts – less cloche and more cap – or romantic, wide brims, such as this pale turquoise 'crinoline' straw (dyed horsehair or jute fibre plaited to give a see-through effect) in a flat, plate style (they were called 'Pamela' hats), about 22 inches across and decorated with self-coloured ribbon and bunch of artificial flowers. These fancy straws were often worn for garden-parties – or by bridesmaids. It's a bit battered and needs a gentle steam to revive. 1930-35. 1930s hats, although not littering the streets, are to be found at fairly reasonable prices: £10-20/$17-33.

SLEEVELESS, CLOSE-FITTING and very slinky dance dress in silver lamé and lime green in wide, vertical stripes cut on the bias, the back cut to a deep 'v' and a cowled front at the neck. There is a flying panel of the same material attached to one shoulder. Fastens with hooks and eyes at the side. Dress-maker made. Fair condition. £30-40/$50-66. (See Plate 5.)

This is 'strictly ball-room' and the bee's knees for all classes of young (and slightly older) things in the early Thirties.

ANOTHER SHAMELESS SLINKY DRESS, this time in a 'burnt orange' shade, the material a wondrous, spongy, silk crêpe (*cloque*) that has a lot of 'give' (a good thing since there are no fastenings on this dress – you just wriggled into it). The neckline is a shallow 'v' with fine gathers, gauged across the bosom, while the back (the newly discovered erogenous zone of the era) has deep 'cut outs', shoulder straps to waist. I doubt you could have worn anything beneath the dress, apart from a dab of scent. I bet her mother thought it was positively indecent. Superbly dress-maker made. No label. Classic, timeless, lovely. **£40-55 / $66-90.**

MORE HEADY GLITZ and glamour in a very fine pleated black silk and lace 'Teddy' – the American version of camiknickers. It has narrow, shoe-string straps, with a wickedly sexy panel of black lace inserted at the front and sides. At the back is a small, centre opening which fastens with three teeny dark pearl buttons. Delicious. All professionally hand sewn. No label, but without hesitation I'd say 'Made in France' – and so would you. Truly romantic and could be worn now. I must show this off to the vicar on a future occasion. **£60-70 / $100-115.**

TEDDIES

The difference between a 'Teddy' and camiknickers is that a Teddy has no fiddly buttons to cope with 'down there' – you simply step into it and originally it was called a 'step-in'. I am told (by an American) the name 'Teddy' was acquired because it's a garment that 'loves to hug you'. You can't argue with that.

YET ANOTHER SLEEVELESS evening gown, this time *haute couture*. Made of cerise-coloured, bias-cut silk velvet, sleek as a cat, worn with a long-sleeved bolero. Edged across the neck and round the sleeves with a deep, encrusted braid of sequins in a burnished silvery gold, which is repeated at the front hem. It fastens at the side with a heavy metal zip, not used on women's clothes before the Thirties. The bolero is very dramatic and Spanish looking, with padded sleeve-heads and covered with more of this dazzling spangled braid. If you turn the dress inside out, you see that only the side seams are machine stitched – all else is hand sewn and the raw edges completely over-sewn to stop the material unravelling. The strength of the finish and detailed care, apart from the design, is the skill of 'top' dress-making. The label, unobtrusive in the side seam, states: 'Eva Lutyens London'. I have now started a quest to find out more about this designer, about whom there is little documented. Her work is similar to any of the 'greats' of the period – Schiaparelli, Chanel, Patou. A lovely dress. I adore looking at her and, naturally, I call her 'Carmen'. About 1938. **£100-150/$165-248 upwards.** (*See Plate 5.*)

PAIR OF GOLD KID court shoes, for evening wear, with 2-inch heels. The prettiest little pair of shoes. Label: 'Lilley and Skinner Ltd.' About 1938. **£20/$33.** (*See Plate 5.*)

PERHAPS I'D BETTER LOWER the temperature with a long, yellow under-vest, hand knitted in a 'drop-stitch', lacey pattern with silky yarn (artificial, called 'Luvisca') that has a distinct 'sheen' to it. Vests are very British: there are lots of home-knit vests in the collection, some, like this one, coloured, also in pink, green, blue. My yellow one is in mint condition, apparently unworn. **£5/$8.**

ROLL-ON GIRDLE MADE FROM loomed elastic (which first appeared in the late 1920s) and increasingly popular with young women during the 1930s. Most of the ones you find now are probably from the 1940s and 1950s – the pattern didn't change very much – but they're usually in a very bad state of decay. Day by day, they did a tough job well, keeping tummies in, bottoms flat, holding stockings up and, if necessary, tucking vests down. All this effort wore them out. **50p-£2/80 cents-$3.**

ABRASSIÈRE THAT, AT LAST, looks more convincingly like one we can recognize. Separate cups that work on the theory of 'round 'em up and head 'em out'. The bra, made from black 'washing silk' is unstructured (no hard bits), with elastic straps that criss-cross the back and then button under the bust cups. It has ribbon shoulder-straps with adjusting slides. Label: 'Kestos Highline Brassiere'. Bras like this one are getting scarce. In good condition. 1930s. **£20/$33 upwards.**

The Kestos (designed by a woman) was the famous bra of the late 1920s and 1930s as it was just the job under the lighter, easier clothes of the time and was especially good under knitwear.

HERE COMES THE BRIDE OF 1939. Palest pink, slim-fitted gown with skirt widening into a long train. The fabric is incredible! The basis is a delicate, spider's web net which is covered with flossed-silk 'spaghetti' braid in a continuous flowing pattern of swirls and curves. The long, tight sleeves, with slightly 'squared' shoulders, have self-

covered buttons to decorate the wrists (I always think 'same material' buttons are an elegant detail). The dress is designed with a high neck, a sewn-in pink satin slip and fastens with poppers and hooks-and-eyes at the side. The train, which stretches out for about 4 or 5 feet, is under-pinned with ripples of pink net frills.

WITH IT, THIS LUCKY BRIDE wore a simple, wired head-dress of pale pink silk leaves and pearls, all bound with silver thread. Also in the box were a pair of 3-inch heeled pink silk, round-toed court shoes, size 6, marked inside 'Creation of Saxone Shoe Co Ltd.' Also a pair of sheer silk stockings in the same pleasing shade, marked: 'Bondor Ringclear. British Made. Patented Licence No... Genuine 3 Carrier' (which denotes the weight of silk). The late 1930s produced some exceptionally fine bridal array, of which mine is an example, and it's in wonderful condition. The box that it came in is marked: 'Elizabeth Court dressmaker, 42-44 Pitt Street, Edinburgh'. **£250/$412 the ensemble.**

PALE PINK, ORIENTAL SILK 2-piece pyjamas decorated with insertions and appliqués of embroidered net. Tunic top made with shoulder straps and low-cut neck and back. Two small pockets at the hips and an attached tie belt. The wide-legged trousers (26 inches at the ankle) flare from a side-buttoning hip yoke. Professionally hand sewn. Made in either Hong Kong or Singapore. Good condition. Very attractive and feminine and nice to wear. 1930-35. **£75/$122 upwards.**

POSSIBLY WORN OVER pyjamas at breakfast, a magnolia-coloured crêpe de Chine, kimono-style wrapper, with wide sleeves decorated with embroidered cut-work. Again, brilliantly hand sewn in an elegant design and originating from Hong Kong or Singapore. **£40/$66 upwards.**

PYJAMAS

Pyjamas (originating in India and the East) had started off, for women, in about 1914 as sleep-suits and were made in warm materials. By the late 1920s, designed in silks and chiffons, they became witty, slip-into-something-sensational beach into cocktail hour 'lounge' wear for rich women who holidayed in the sun. Pyjamas, imbued with this film-star status, next eased their way down the social scale in the 1930s and turned into decorative and sexy bed-wear for bright young things everywhere.

A HEAVY SILK SATIN, deep peachy-pink night-dress, bias cut with straps that tie on the shoulders with bows. The bodice front is entirely made from a section of net with appliquéd cut-outs of the satin. Professionally hand sewn. Made in Malta. Good condition. 1930-35. **£40/ $66 up-wards.**

T HEY DID HAVE OTHER COLOURS beside pink. There was lots of white (cotton as well as silks) and many other pastel hues. Very full-skirted nightdress in mauvey-blue 'georgette' (a dense chiffon crêpe) with deep, frilled, *elasticated* armholes that help to give a ruched effect to the bodice. Self-belt loops at the waist hold a very long violet-coloured sash with matching bows on the shoulders. Neatly hand sewn in an unusual style from material from Liberty & Co. 1935. **£30-35/$50-58.**

NIGHTDRESSES

I have five nightdresses from this same batch, all made with Liberty materials and all superb. Quite honestly, they look like evening dresses. They were made by the artistic sister of the original owner, who told me that when you were invited to stay at large country houses for the weekend, you needed to make sure that your weekending wardrobe, including nightwear, was up to the mark, since the servants who unpacked and put out your clothes could tell 'who was and who wasn't' by the quality of your unmentionables. In future, please bear that in mind when you go to stay with elegant friends.

FURS

I know these are now a horror story, but they represent an entire area of costume history which we can't easily ignore. Fur pieces of all kinds – stoles, tippets, capes, cuffs, muffs, bags, gloves and trims, as well as fur coats – were fashionable and universally worn by all classes between the Wars. Without the addition of a fox-fur stole, with mask and paws, you were not a dedicated follower of fashion in the Thirties. Indeed, noted in the list of wedding gifts to H.R.H. Princess Marina of Kent in 1934 are several furs, including a fox-fur cape. If you are brave and buy one for your collection (and at the moment I would say that costume dealers, and everyone else, are *giving* them away), make sure it is clean and in no way being attacked by moth or other insects. Such infestation can wreak havoc within the confines of a costume room (I know, because I've had experience of this). My advice is to put the fox in a plastic bag and pop it in the freezer for an hour or two – that should do the trick of bumping off any wildlife. Don't leave it in the plastic, though. Best to shove it into an old cotton pillow-slip with a couple of moth balls or a lavender bag for company.

EARLY PLASTIC/COMPOSITION costume jewellery – including belt buckles – were often in great Art Deco designs. A wonderful and inexpensive area for collecting, as a timeless, flexible snake bangle shows. The design could be found in Ancient Egypt; it's sinuous form was also admired by the Neo-classicals, sentimentalized by the Victorians, eroticized in art nouveau designs and still enjoyed during the Art Deco period. It is the symbol of eternity – thus girls still keep a snake up their arm. Gilt, spiral snake. **£6/$10.**

THERE ARE SO MANY bits and pieces that belong, quite naturally, to the 1930s, such as the coatee, absolutely the in thing. Coatees were easy to make, short, edge-to-edge jackets, either plain or (for evening) fancy. Here's a quote from *The Lady's Companion*, a weekly magazine, from May 1934: 'When a cool evening ends a hot summer's day, it's nice to have a little coatee to slip on over your thin frock, isn't it? We show you the very design – both businesslike in style and easy to run up. Make it in velveteen.' Since there must have been thousands and thousands 'run up' I think you're bound to strike lucky and find one in a vintage clothes shop or somewhere. **£8-30/$13-50 plus depending on style, material and making.**

KNITWEAR

Rarer to find in good condition would be the 'Knitwear for Yourself and Hubby' also described in *The Lady's Companion*. But do look out for interesting hand-knits, such as separate collars, considered very jolly for the next thirty years. Shop bought, plain or fancy, they could be made of anything – crisp piqué, embroidered organdie or lace. Puritan, Etonian, Cedric Fauntleroy or Peter Pan, all there to perk up a tired dress. Very pretty to look at and still cheap to buy. Also look for false flowers – good quality, wired artificial flowers (orchids very popular) that often sprout a bit of fern as well.

MEN'S UNDERWEAR 1930

F OR MY 1930S TAIL PIECE here he is – in a pair of absolutely mind-blowingly smart under-drawers. Duck-egg blue cashmere trunks with fine ribbed waistband and leg ends. 22 inches long with 'fully fashioned' fit at crotch. Excellent condition. Unworn and boxed. Label: 'Edouard & Butler, Hosiers and Shirtmakers, 15d Clifford Street, Bond Street, London'. The owner's initials are embroidered in red: 'R.E.B.' This is the most elegant pair of gentlemen's pants I have ever clapped eyes on. Surely Rhett Butler himself? £30/$50 for the definitive glamorous knight?

THE 1940s MAKE DO AND MEND

I have a suspicion that the prevailing image of 1940s clothes is dowdy and, certainly during the Second World War, drab and distinctly not directed by fashion. Nothing could be further from the truth. You have only to look at copies of *Vogue* from the 1940s to see that throughout the War there were still very beautiful clothes to be bought – if you had the money and knew where to go. Although these were distinct advantages to being well dressed, the point is that all the glamour, glitz, beauty and know-how of the 1930s didn't just disappear between autumn 1939 and summer 1945; rather, it was on hold, treading water, waiting for the

re-emergence that came after the War ended. If anything, the cinema-led inspiration of the previous decade became even more insistent during the 1940s.

From 1942, when Government rationing really took hold, ordinary, manufactured clothes began to be in short supply – clothing coupons had to be surrendered to obtain even the most basic garments. Every sort of simple component needed to make clothes was likely to be on the 'restricted use' list, harnessed for the War Effort, and thus there were very few new outfits. Most people had to re-invent what clothing they had. Material of any sort was eked out in the most economic way and clothes manufactured under the 'Utility CC41' (Civilian Clothing 1941) label were designed and made to strict Board of Trade regulations. No fuss, no waste, that was the message. But women (because they are forever optimistic and inventive) still got out their pins and scissors and bashed away on old sewing-machines and made all manner of wonderful clothes out of any bits and pieces of cloth they could lay hands on. I'm always hearing from ladies how particular effort was made to get something new to wear when 'he' was due home on leave. Adversity often aids artistic endeavour, and ingenious notions sprang into being under these 'waste not, want not' years.

I was born in 1940, so I can just remember how the War years felt and have vague recollections of my mother's clothes. Now I realize they all dated from the

1930s and, after the War, she couldn't wait to cast them aside. Their wearing had gone on too long and the memories they held were, possibly, too painful.

Certainly, it wasn't all doom and gloom, so I'm going to have a good old search about in the Costume Room and see what nostalgic pieces I can find to describe. One of the problems with the 1940s – as I am always telling my students – is the scarcity of complete outfits because, naturally, everything either wore out or was 'altered' or made over in some way. What you do tend to find is a lot of hard-wearing clothes, especially coats (you needed a warm top covering in the cold winters of the 1940s) and these have lasted the years, often relegated to dog-walking or gardening wear. But, for the rest, clothes usually became rag rugs or bonfire fodder... especially after the 'New Look' was launched in 1947.

Christian Dior was forty-two when he took Paris by storm with his first collection for the House of Dior. A quiet, middle-class, slightly plump, cultured gentleman who had wanted to be an architect, he was an unlikely candidate for a revolutionary. But, in essence, he was just that. He was inspired by the voluptuous beauty of Victorian and Edwardian clothes – the sort his grandmother and mother had worn – so, as a tonic for women dressed in the severe, short, material-starved garments of the recent past, he created lovely, graceful gowns and costumes for his debut. Dior's hemlines dipped to eight inches from the ground, hips were padded and waists were small so that the skirts sprang into sweeping arcs. The sumptuousness of these clothes, although politically incorrect in post-War Europe, brought gasps of wonder and excitement from the buyers and fashion journalists who first packed into that salon on a freezing winter's day. Here was not just new fashion, but a new woman. The master's skirts were long, full and, famously, pleated, thus doubling the yardage required. This delicious extravagance furiously outraged some, but pleased cloth merchants (on both sides of the Channel), and although very few had a real Dior in 1947, it was this flamboyant disregard for economic realities that entranced all women. It was pure romance. Petticoats had returned. The New Look was love at first sight; Dior appealed to a basic instinct – lady, be a dame!

CLOTHES OF THE 1940S

It's Spring, and as I'm running up the stairs I realize how dirty the house is looking. Rather than writing about the charm of old clothes, I ought to be cleaning this old house. The trouble is, housework's always there waiting to be done again; it's such a dreadful waste of energy. But, poetically, the sight of daffodils stirs latent tremors within me and, though quickly subdued, I can't help feeling a twang of guilt as the sun points out the dusty corners, grubby paintwork and dog's hair on the carpets. (My son-in-law is always afflicted with dreadful sneezing and wheezing on entering this house and has to live, like a recluse, in the dog-free drawing-room.) I cannot think what brought all this to mind, apart from seeing the dirty paint clearly because I had my glasses on – usually I leave them downstairs. Anyway, to more interesting matters: I have found, for your further delight and for an understanding of the 1940s, the items below.

> Lent and Easter in a vicarage can be very harrowing. Yes, it's a time of reflection, preparation, self-denial, Bible study and Holy Thoughts, etc., but, oh boy, the vicar gets so up-tight because he's at the end of his tether, writing dozens of sermons and doing all those extra services, having decided, for various Proper Reasons, to give up alcohol for the duration. It's a mistake in my opinion; indeed, I suspect that after Easter most Church of England parsons are probably reeling around in a state of complete inebriation, thankful to have got through the torment for yet another year.

This Mr. Fenwick is the same gentleman who opened the posh shop in Bond Street in 1891, but the Newcastle shop – a most exclusive establishment – came first, in 1882.

A KNEE-LENGTH, 'SQUARE LOOK' winter coat in herringbone tweed mix of green/black/maroon with pockets and button-to belt. Lined with brown twilled wool. Label: 'Mr. J. J. Fenwick. Court Dressmaker, Ladies Tailor and Furrier. Newcastle on Tyne'. Some damage to material, but what a 'quality' coat! About 1940. **£40-50/$66-82.**

Dress made from a heavy linen-look material. In dark maroon with a vertical lime green stripe, it has short sleeves, sweetheart neckline, has lost its belt and has a heavy metal zip at the side. It's shop bought. Very smart in its day. About 1942. **£15-20/$25-33**.

Pair of black suede and snakeskin shoes, sling-back, 4-inch wedge heel with peep-toe. There were a lot of sexy peeping toes about at this time, especially attractive if you still had a bit of red lacquer to paint the nails with. These shoes have no maker's mark. Beautiful workmanship, but very heavy. Good condition. About 1943. **£2/$3 upwards**.

Shoes

Everybody thinks of 'wedge' shoes for the 1940s. All shoes from the War years tend to be well made and sturdy, some might say clompy, but they are dainty compared to, say, the Vivienne Westwood totter-downs available today.

Here is a pair of brown brogue (originally meaning a strong, low-cut leather shoe for country wear), lace-up shoes with sturdy heels of stacked leather. Label: 'K shoes'. About 1940. **£25/$40**. (*See Plate 6.*)

Zips

You can always tell really early zips because they look as though they could do up seamen's boots and leather luggage – and that's what they did around 1900. Be different, look out for lonely old zips; they use always to be saved, unpicked from worn clothes and stripped out of old bags to re-use because, of course, new metal zips were not available during the War and, in any case, were expensive. The early ones are often brass, have huge teeth, never go wrong and possibly have 'Lightning' on the pull. You can also find dresses from the 1930s with large 'Bakelite' (an early plastic) zips, which in turn were first called the 'Lightning' fastener. Zippers gotta lotta history.

A SHIRRED ELASTIC, TWO-PIECE bathing costume, home-made from red and white Rayon crêpe (it had been a 1930s dress). Simple, halter bra-top and big knickers, which are very clever, stretching happily from a size 10 to a generous 14. Much worn (and loved). It was made just after the War by a woman who loved the idea of the two-piece. She said it was better than a shop-bought bikini because you could have the pants, as she said, 'up or down, according to the weather'. How useful! 1947. **£5/$8**.

MAKESHIFT BATHERS

Adding to the theme of bathing costumes, I have a letter from my friend Christine in Mirfield, Yorkshire and she encloses a photograph of her in a two-piece swimsuit (1943) made out of an old woollen jumper. The sleeves and top half were used for the bra and the cut-off bottom part became the pants. She says: 'We then traced and embroidered the names of American States (popular with the Yanks).' Chris looks a billion dollars in hers and appears to have Ohio on her bust. Necessity is the mother of invention.

A HANDSOME, RED, FOX FUR, knee-length coat worked in verticals and collarless. Square, padded shoulders with widening sleeves (that are faced with lining silk on the inner side to help with the shaping and lessen the 'rub' on the fur). The lining is also beautifully decorated with patterned ribbon-work. No maker's label. Probably from America or Canada. 1940-47. At a time when you can't seem to give old furs away, I paid **£75/$122** for it two years ago because it was such a beautiful example of furrier's art.

T OFFEE BROWN, FELT HAT with peak (looks like an officer's 'cheese-cutter'). Celia Johnson wore one just like it in *Brief Encounter* and looked sensational. About 1943. **£20-25/$33-40**. (See Plate 6.) Also, a red and white, hand-knitted, 'dart-board' beret with tassel. **£4/$7**.

HATS

There were the most amazingly beautiful, cute, witty hats made throughout the War, both hats 'off coupons' and, of course, many which were homemade. A new hat, at a time when women wore them daily, gave a definite boost to the morale. I'm sure that's why people now love watching the War years costume dramas on television. It's all the wonderful hats!

HAT MADE OF MAROON felt in a forage cap style with nape-band and cheeky self-bow on top. It lives in a square, black hat box labelled 'Mr. J. J. Fenwick' in white letters. The coat and hat came into the collection via different people, but, incredibly, they go well together. 1940s. Hat and box together: £30/$50.

HERE ARE THREE very different hats. Small straw trilby trimmed with a pheasant feather and a bright red, curly feather. American. About 1946. £45-50/$72-82. Small, damson velvet, soft-crowned, 'chimney pot' hat, trimmed with yellow feather. American. 1946-48. £50/$82 upwards. Bright blue felt trilby trimmed with petersham ribbon. 1940-45. (See Plate 6.)

THESE ARE SCRUMPTIOUS. You'd love them. Pair of very, very dark brown suede, chunky, 2-inch heeled shoes with peep toes and three small, buckled straps on the uppers, edged with brown silk braid. Beautifully made. CC41 Utility Mark. Embossed inside: 'Town Walkers Lilley & Skinner Ltd. London'. Smart art, and very comfy. Good condition (they're my size, too, a 5). £24/$42. (See also Plate 6.)

These shoes are illustrated to the left below.

DAY-WEAR SHOES with ankle straps and chunky heels, slight platforms and sexy peeping toes. Made from sturdy black calf with 'reptile' trim. Dyed pale blue inside. No maker's label, but there is a 'CC41' marked at the back. Very good condition. 1947-50. £45-55/$72-90.

SMALL, RED-LIDDED, round pot of rouge with Yardley 'Bee' motif on the lid. Tiny bottle of 'Cutex' nail powder polish. Red cotton handkerchief, white embroidered 'Pour le Rouge' in one corner; card of 'Dinkie' hair clips; powder

These are the sort of things you would have found inside a hand-bag in the 1940s.

compact, round, brown leather, with stud fastening and a printed picture of two horses on the lid, still full of very pink powder (looks like brick dust) but smelling instantly of my mother and grandmother. Another silk crêpe hanky with a picture of Marlene Dietrich in one corner. All these things are not expensive in themselves – a few pence to a few pounds – but they are atmospheric and fascinating.

ZIPPERED, CIRCULAR HANDBAG, 10 inches across, commercially made from brown crocheted cord with lovely 'Prystal' (early plastic) amber-coloured twist-ring handles and decorative tassel on zip. Cloth lined. Good condition. Likely made in USA. **£35-40 / $58-66**. Also, small, punt-shaped wicker shopping basket with sturdy handle. 1940. **£12 / $20**. (*See Plate 6.*)

A CHOKER NECKLACE made from clear glass beads in bright primary colours with screw clasp. They look like playground marbles, but actually this is classic jewellery of the 1940s. **£12 / $20**.

LONG, NARROW, FRINGED MUFFLER, machine knitted in autumnal colours in a zig-zag pattern with Art Deco overtones. 1940-45. **£12-15 / $20-25**. (*See Plate 6.*)

The Arbiter of Good Taste exclaimed with disbelief when she spied the next garment draped casually across my desk. The fact that any of my 'old' things could look quite so acceptably now amazed her.

PAIR OF HAND-CROCHETED camiknickers – absolutely beautifully made – in a bright, raspberry pink, silky yarn. They are superb. A knockout. The crochet is very fine and intricate (bet it was a 'Stitchcraft' pattern) so that the whole cami is light and stretchy. Three substantial pearl buttons do it up underneath. And, now, of course, crochet is all the ton once more. It was given to me by a lady who said it proved that not all the undies of the 1940s were passion killers. Bless her. About 1945. **£30-35 / $50-58**.

STRIPED TWO-PIECE IN lime green, orange, lemon and brown artificial silk. Button-through summer dress with pockets, knee length and worn over a matching one-piece (shorts and halter-neck) sun or 'play' suit. Pretty and well made with large, self-covered buttons and the halter has the self-loops at the back. Goodness, they did love those fiddly loops to do up, didn't they? Professionally sewn. Machined and hand finished. 1940-50. **£45/$75**. Looks the business with a big, heavy-plaited straw sun-hat. **£25/$40**.

DRESS MADE OF RAYON, with a repeated design in vibrant blues, pinks, yellows and greens on a black background. Shortish sleeves, high round neck, fastening on each shoulder with 5 buttons and self-loops. Original belt missing (but I use a black patent with it). Very smart. Nice condition. Dress-maker made. 1940-46. **£35/$58**.

This is the sort of thing lots of ladies used to put on in the afternoon to go out to tea or to a Women's Institute meeting.

SILK AFTERNOON DRESS with leather belt and puff sleeves in a vivid red, blue, green, yellow and white 'spattered' and floral pattern on a black ground. It is to the knee with two short pleats, front and back. American. About 1945. **£35/$58**. (*See Plate 6.*)

MOLL THE DUMMY

I have one extremely useful dress-maker's dummy that stands in my study when I'm writing, and I can fling anything on her in order to get an idea. She's so accommodating that I call her 'Moll'. Moll doesn't mind what she wears; basically she's a curvey size 10 (she was 'moulded' in the 1880s) and she looks good in anything, even though she has a distinct lean to one side. It's easier to have a shape inside the clothes when you're studying them – so my advice, Collector Person, would be to get yourself a dummy if you can. You do see them in junk/antique shops but, if you want a new one, contact Siegel and Stockman (*see p.187*), who make the finest dress forms in the world. Moll is doing her Greer Garson act as I write...

PAIR OF BLACK SILK FISH-NET stockings. Perfect apart from heavily darned toes (was the original owner a toe dancer, I wonder?). Remember, my dears, legs look their best in fish-nets, like faces under veils. **£3/$5.**

Damaged parachutes (either silk or nylon, which was invented by American chemists just before the War) were released by the military for civilian use and were 'off coupons'.

WHITE NYLON NIGHTDRESS trimmed with coarse cream lace. Hand sewn and homemade from the gleanings of a parachute. Lots of underwear and other garments were made from these off-cuts, some of which were coloured. The nightdress still has the 'chute seams criss-crossing the skirt. One bit stamped 'A.N' – American Navy. Probably never worn (it was hot stuff, in every sense) but very interesting. About 1945. **£10/$17.**

A PAIR OF FRENCH-STYLE knickers (with loop to hang them up by) and matching slip made in shiny pink Rayon satin with a tiny flower pattern. Plain apart from a bit of frill across the bosom (or 'chest' as my old aunts said) Label: 'Polychord Design & Make. CC41'. Unworn. About 1948. **£12/$20.**

AN APRON THAT WAS POSSIBLY made at the suggestion of the Board of Trade's helpful hinter, 'Mrs Sew and Sew'. It is shield shaped with a frilled edging created from a silk map. Strangely enough, many maps were printed on stiffened silk, originally intended for lightweight carriage. They could be bought from bookshops for about half a crown (12½ pence), soaked to loosen the glue, washed and re-used. My apron shows Borneo, Sumatra and Java, and part of French Indo-China has been used on the ties. Unusual. About 1942. **£28/$46.**

ANOTHER POWDER COMPACT – a whopper (they got larger and larger during the 1940s because of the emphasis on a 'film star' face). Round, gold metal, 4 inches across with

just a bit of restrained engine-turning, back and front. It's in its original felt case, but the best thing, on the lid, in the centre medallion, is the engraving: '1948. To Ivy Love Arthur'. Isn't that lovely? It's been well used, too. Buckets of scented brick-dust. Maker: 'Pygmalion'. **£25/$40.**

A TWO-HANDLED, GREEN, box-shaped hand-bag in pretend suede with zipper fastening the top. The bottom layer pulls out, like a drawer, and contains a gas-mask. About 1940. These camouflaged gas containers are to be found if you hunt – often they are made in smart leather – but a manufactured, cheap 'fashion' one like this is very rare. **£20/$33 upwards.**

B UTTERICK PAPER DRESS-MAKING pattern of a smart 'town' dress with patch pockets and 'simulated bolero'. Marked: '2/9 plus Purchase Tax'. The packet also printed with the warning: 'Professional dressmakers are reminded that they must comply with the making of Civilian Clothing (restriction) Orders'. About 1943. **50p-£1/80 cents-$1.65.**

D AY DRESS WITH RED, long-sleeved bodice and slightly flared, black skirt. Made from Rayon crêpe. This two-tone effect is typical of the 'square', masculine look of the War years. The shoulders are padded and the dress, with short lapels, fastens like a double-breasted jacket with large red and black buttons. It has a dummy top pocket complete with hanky. Original belt missing, but I have added a narrow black patent one. It's a smart get-up. Dress-maker made. **£28/$46.**

A GREEN WOOLLY CARDIGAN in rib and cable stitch and fronted with rows of vertical 'bobbles', interspersed with embroidered flowers in bright colours. 6 large green buttons. It has been used hard but was very well knitted. Quite possibly re-cycled wool. Woollen garments were unpicked, the wool washed and then re-used. About 1940. **20p/40 cents upwards.**

Everyone could knit; what else could you do in an air-raid shelter? No, don't answer that.

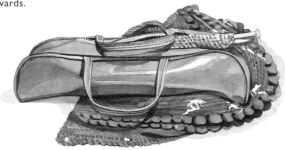

H IP-LENGTH, HORIZONTAL STRIPED, machine-knitted wool cardigan/jacket in shades of grey, brick red, black, yellow and green, fashioned to fit snug to the waist. It has padded shoulders, two pockets and fastens, from the waist, with six pearly grey buttons. Label: 'The Knitwear House, Huppert Ltd. Regent Street'. Huppert did beautiful knitwear and blouses. This is such a smart jacket that you'd go 'ooh' if you saw it and it would look fashionable even now. 1947-50. **£40/$66 upwards.** (*See Plate 6.*)

C LASSIC, ELEGANT, KNEE-LENGTH, black crêpe and lace, short-sleeved cocktail/dinner dress. The black lace is used only on the bodice and sleeves, overlaid by criss-crossed bands of the dense crêpe in a lattice pattern (very complicated to do), but it looks most effective worn over its original peach pink slip. Fastens at side with press-studs. Beautifully dress-maker made. 1940-50. **£35/$58.**

F RENCH GREY, FINE TWILLED WOOL, princess-line coat. This is the nearest thing to a pure New Look that I have in the collection. We still had rationing after the War had ended, so lavish amounts of material were not generally available. It still has square, padded shoulders but the line is now much longer; the skirt, with its hidden hip pockets, comes below mid-calf. Double-breasted with two black and silver buttons placed horizontally to emphasize the nipped-in waist. Excellent tailoring. Lined throughout with fawn Rayon. English. Bought and worn by the original owner in 1948. **£40-50/$66-82.** (*See Plate 6.*)

M AROON CALF COURT SHOES (to go with above coat). Rounded toes, very solid 4-inch heels. Nice condition. **£25/$40.** Also part of the original *ensemble*, maroon plastic zip-fastened bag with shoulder strap. (*See Plate 6.*)

I have done another sort through the Costume Room to see what else gives the right 'tone' for the Forties. The dog insisted on bringing his ball with him and kept dropping it into a large box of shoes I was trying to look through: he thinks this is a game I have a passion for. It thus takes more time to sort out my stuff, but I don't like to appear insensitive to his doggy kindness. Arms loaded, I trail downstairs once more.

PAIR OF NAVY BLUE, chalk-striped 'slacks', 10 inches wide at the turn-ups. Made from men's suiting; two pockets and side-button fastening. Slacks are difficult to find in good condition. No label. About 1940. £38/$63.

Hey, women in trousers — the Modern Girl kicks in!

MUSTARD YELLOW, cap-sleeved, close-fitting sweater, hand knitted in 4 pearl, 4 plain rib in a heavy silky yarn, with 3 pearl buttons. About 1940. £8-10/$13-17.

SWEATER GIRLS

The sweater was the most popular garment during the War. In Hollywood, Lana Turner was the original 'Sweater Girl', Ann Sheridan was known as the 'Oomph Girl' and eventually Jane Russell, starring in the film *The Outlaw*, was to go to the top of the class as the Girl with the Most Beautiful Breasts. I remember thinking, as a schoolgirl watching that film, that her bosom never went floppy like those of the other ladies I saw. How observant can you get!

TWO-PIECE 'COSTUME' (as my mother still called them in the 1940s and 1950s) in brown/fawn Prince of Wales check woollen cloth. The jacket is cut with small, unflappable revers, sternly padded shoulders, inverted pockets, three horn buttons to a single-breasted fastening and lined with biscuit coloured silk. The skirt is box pleated and to the knee. These 'no nonsense' suits, directly descended from the walking suits of the late nineteenth century, are still worn even now in rural areas. Get one and treasure it. They never wear out, they never cease to be in fashion. Label: 'Boughy. Tailor. Shrewsbury'. About 1940. £30-35/$50-58. (*See Plate 6.*)

The style of this suit is 'Good Ladies of the Shires' and totally 'Miss Marple'. I enjoy traditional walking-suits like this because they have such character.

TO GO WITH THE SUIT, a brown lizardskin, snap-frame handbag (10 × 6 inches). Re-handled, battered but still highly polished. Mappin and Webb and others of that ilk have done bags like this forever. 1940s onwards. £5/$8.

RED SUEDE DOROTHY BAG constructed on an extending brass frame with interior purse. About 1940. £20-30/$33-50. (*See Plate 1.*)

BROOCH, HANDMADE FROM red stitched black felt in the shape of a tiny hat and handbag swinging from a bow. About 1940. £3/$5.

PINK TWO-PIECE MADE FROM 'Moygashel' – the jacket vaguely 'out of Africa'-looking with button-down patch pockets and short sleeves. The skirt is knee length with a few unpressed pleats. Label: 'Treesha'. About 1950. **£25-30/$40-50**. It's the sort of thing my mother wore in summer with white buck-skin shoes (that had to be whitened and dried before we went out). 1940. **£20/$33**. (*See Plate 7.*)

My donor here has popped a note into the pocket to say when the raincoat was worn. This makes all the difference to a collection.

RED (ARDENTLY THE COLOUR OF THE 1940S) Rayon gaberdine raincoat, double-breasted, belted, with large pockets and a detachable hood. Lined with shiny brown 'slipper' satin. Label: 'Asta Model'. There's one like this advertised in the American Sears' Catalog for 1947/8: 'Hoods are Newest Fashion Additions to Any-Weather Coats'. Condition, rather worn. 1949. **£20/$33 upwards**.

CIRCULAR, BANDBOX EVENING purse (6 inches wide) on a loop handle, made of black satin embroidered with oriental symbols (chrysanthemums and cranes). Interior with fixed looking-glass. About 1940. **£30/$50**.

SCARVES

Scarves are the most emotive accessories of the 1940s. You can imagine the Wartime factory girls with their crowning glories well secured beneath tall, tightly-tied turbans – film star Carmen Miranda's Latin American answer to Safety First. If you are keen to collect scarves, we now come to some of the most thrilling design years, which saw a great variety of colours and patterns. Some are minor works of art. Looking through my box, it was difficult to choose, but below are two examples, both by Jacqmar, a fashion company who brought out stunning 'propaganda' scarves during the War. (*See Plate 6.*)

HEAVY RAYON SILK CRÊPE (31 × 31 inches) scarf printed with a busy, colourful pub scene – including a soldier, sailor and airman. The centre panel reads: 'Time Gentlemen

– Please'. Around the rolled border are the names of 232 London pubs. Well worn, but still lovely and amusing – humour is one of the best features of 1940s scarves. About 1948. **£12/$20.**

VERY HEAVY SQUARE (33 × 33 inches) of dyed pale blue Rayon/linen printed with British Military Services badges, mostly coloured in gold, green, purple and blue. Around the hand-rolled hem, the repeated phrase: 'Into Battle'. About 1942. **£80/$132.**

HEAVY BLACK SILK CRÊPE, with padded short sleeves: a full length dinner/theatre dress with deep decolleté front and back. The skirt cut in wide panels. The dress is decorated with a large diamond 'pane' of gold beadwork across the front bodice and trails of the same around the neckline and down the centre front of skirt. Heavy metal zip at side and tie belt. No label (sadly). Beautifully designed and made. Very, very sophisticated and Katherine Hepburn looking. Could easily be an American garment since America substituted for France as a dress designer during the War. Classic, wearable. 1945-48. **£80-100/$132-165.**

ANOTHER LOVELY DANCE DRESS made of fire red twilled silk, a strapless sheath with well-boned bodice in a cascade design of horizontal pleats. Lined and with a self-belt. Absolutely scrumptious. Label: 'Harvey Nichols. London'. I suspect that it is a designer dress (maybe Norman Hartnell or Victor Steibel), bought in as a sample by Harvey Nichols and therefore displaying their own label. It's very Rita Hayworth. 1948. **£40/$66.**

The lady who sold me this told me that she saw this dress and just yearned to have it and paid for it bit by pay-day bit because she knew it was a dress in a million.

BOTH THESE DRESSES could be worn with this pair of gold and silver, pleated leather, platform, peep-toed evening shoes with 4-inch heels (women really took to higher ground with the New Look) and ankle straps. Very Princess Margaret – even more so since they are made by 'Rayne' and have the Royal Warrant stamped in silver on the inside. Good condition. 1948-50. **£35/$58.** (*See Plate 7.*)

DINNER DRESS OF PURPLE silk velvet with padded shoulders, sweetheart neckline, bias-cut skirt and bracelet length, puckered and gauged sleeves. Side fastening with lots of poppers. Well made (all the seams oversewn). The dress of a well-to-do matron. Label: 'Debenham and Freebody, London'. Good condition. 1948-50. **£75-80/$122-132.**

TYPICAL 2-INCH DIAMOND paste brooch that divides into two dress-clips. These were an attractive way to 'finish' a neckline – and also to hold an errant strap in place. About 1940. **£15-20/$25-33.**

ENVELOPE CLUTCH HANDBAG (12 × 8 inches) made in strips of scarlet and navy felt in a basket-weave design. Homemade to a magazine pattern in 1943. **£15/ $25.**

A PAIR OF 15-DENIER nylon stockings in a pale tan shade with black seams, heel and sole outlined in black. Picot-edged welt marked: 'First Quality. Du Pont'. Unworn. Rare. About 1940. **£20/$33 upwards.**

NYLONS

Every girl wanted a pair of nylon stockings, the bench-mark of luxury that made you feel a star the minute you put them on, especially after all the old wrinkly Rayon – not to mention socks and gravy browning. Stocks of nylons were non-existent in this country until the late 1940s, but a few magic pairs were imported via the American and Canadian G.I.s stationed here.

TWO LARGE BUTTERFLY BROOCHES painted in dazzling green, red, black and white markings under a layer of plastic. They are quite lovely and these I often wear. Very 1940s. Not worth a fortune, but just *superb* design. Look out for the fashion jewellery that was made during this time in all kinds of unusual materials.

MEN'S UNDERWEAR OF THE 1940S

THE MAN OF THE TIME wore this pair of old, yellowing, wollen lock-knit jersey trunks (22-inch leg) with reinforced cotton waistband and loops for braces. Khaki plastic buttons to close waist. Label: 'WARNORM'. (I have to admit that, in spite of his historic associations, soft, cuddly and well-worn Norm would make the most splendid duster.) Also heavy wool lock-knit vest with short sleeves and 3-button closure at front neck. Label: 'St. Margaret. Mens. CC41'. 1940s. **£10/$17 upwards.**

THE 1950S VOGUE VERSUS BLUE SUEDE SHOES

I have been looking forward to this chapter. The 1950s was my hey-day, so I'm going to be indulgent. I was one of what has been described as the last 'innocent' generation — although I don't think we *meant* to be that innocent. Generally, it was a decade of coming to after the trauma of war, a gathering up of the old skills or trying of new ones, a slow re-adjustment to living with peace. New clothes were important since they were a symbol of optimism. Women (of all classes) wanted to dress up a bit more, especially for going out in the evening (you even dressed smartly to sit in the local picture palace). For women who cared about clothes, France had re-asserted its fashion dictatorship. Paris told you the length to wear your hemline and you obeyed. A copy of *Vogue* was eagerly scanned, even by girls of slender means. It was the lexicon of fashion: 'Buy nothing until you buy *Vogue*' struck deep chords. That best, latest look was sought by lots of ordinary women, although *haute couture* similarity was often achieved via dress-maker patterns on the front-room floor. The other great shopping experience was mail order, which gained more fashion customers during the 1950s.

Ration books were finally abolished in 1952, but there lingered a post-War formality about dressing.

My mother's generation still changed after the morning chores into an 'afternoon frock' and certainly always wore hat and gloves whenever they ventured out to shop. Women expected to get value for money in the clothes they bought. Good quality fabrics and strong stitching (buttons did not fall off in the 1950s) were an accepted feature of clothes bought to last in a way that we never expect or, perhaps, need today. It was the final decade of what my mother would call a well-groomed woman – nowadays that's something you only say about a horse.

Amazingly enough, teenage girls in the early 1950s were usually dressed as miniature versions of their mothers. They wore the same sort of clothes, bought from the same shops, for more or less the same occasions. This was to change dramatically. By the late 1950s, the fashion industry, realizing that the ideal pre-War customer (mature and middle class) no longer had the wherewithal, set its cap at the young and swirled them (and whatever they had to spend) into the excitements of a mass-production concentrated entirely on their sartorial delight. Teenagers trod onto the boards and have never left the stage.

CLOTHES OF THE 1950S

One thing I do notice about the clothes from this decade is that there are a lot of them, and the choice is incredibly varied. The look is either slim as a reed or wide and womanly. Fashion was a booming industry, so, obviously, this increased the range of garments and accessories available and was particularly marked in high street shops. Materials, colours, sizes – the choice accelerates in every area as we move into 'modern' times. If you aim to collect *seriously* only mid- and late twentieth-century clothes (and that's what I'd collect if I were starting now), I advise you to be aware that, ideally, the dress or whatever it is must hold some visual reference that is recognized and identified, maybe uniquely, with the time it was made and used. In other words, it must 'say' something about the era it comes from. Once you get the mass manufactory of the second half of the century then, perforce, you are going to get lots of influences all muddled together. Sort out the wood from the trees. Read all you can about the time in question. Some pieces are vital links in the story chain; others, although amusing or attractive, are red herrings.

> This has been the most trying morning for writing; it has been a day when the vicar has been absent from home due to a school assembly and the Mothers' Union prayers. I have tried several times to go up to the Costume Room, only to be called down again as the door bell peeled or the telephone rang. One parishioner was definitely a bad case of D.A.T.D. (distress at the door), and while I was getting a large hanky and a cup of coffee for this poor soul, the old dog (who is 'in decline', according to the vet) took the opportunity to leg it down the drive and disappear into the churchyard in a twinkling of an eye. In the end I decided to abandon hope until after lunch and try again this afternoon.

Even now, after what is obviously a lot of wear, the whole thing still has an air (on and off the hanger) of being very well-bred, quietly and lastingly

I START WITH MY FAVOURITE suit in the collection from the 1950s (the Arbiter of Good Taste also thinks well of it). It is a narrow, bespoke 2-piece in biscuit-coloured, fine twilled wool with a horizontal shadow stripe, expertly and winningly made. The jacket is 3-buttoned, neat waisted, set with low, wide revers, sloping shoulder line and a padded hip peplum hiding two pockets. The sleeves are narrow with turn back, buttoned cuffs. The mid-calf skirt is pencil slim with flat 'Dior' pleat at the back (a flap of separate material facing a slit, so the outline was elegant but you could walk). There is a lot of hand finish to this garment and the cut and tailoring is superb, but it is essentially very feminine. Label: 'Lachasse'. Lachasse, originally known for 'sporty' clothes, was founded in 1928 and Digby Morton was its first, impeccable designer. After Morton came Hardy Amies and then an elegant Irishman, Michael Donellan, who went on to found his own House. I am certain this suit is by Mr Michael, the Balenciaga of British Couture. About 1950. **£35 / $58 upwards.** (*See Plate 9.*)

chic. In the 1950s, you really still got what you paid for. Classic 2-pieces like this are corner-stones of 1950s dressing, so your collection should have an example.

To balance the slender, reed line, either small, head-hugging hats were worn or plain, 'coolie'-style, large-brimmed efforts. This suit looks entrancing with black accessories such as this plaited wicker hat, 19 inches across brim, with small, shallow crown of dense black nylon. Trimmed with black velvet ribbon and two hat pins. No label. Probably French. **£30-35 / $50-58.** (*See Plate 9.*)

White velvet 'coolie' hat, with 2 wired loops to keep it anchored onto your permed hair, decorated with bunches of fabric violets and plastic lillies-of-the-valley. C & A Modes. About 1953. **£30-35 / $50-58.** (*See Plate 9.*)

Plain, jet black suede court shoes with sturdy, 3-inch heels and high cut, rounded toes. Label: 'Atlas Union Shoe'. **£25-30 / $40-50.** (*See Plate 9.*)

Long (10 × 4 inches) box-shaped bag in black polished calf with self-handle. Inside leather lined, containing looking-glass and gussets for comb, lipstick, etc. (much like the Edwardian travel bag). Heavy gilt twist clasp and hinges. No label – could be American. **£25 / $40.**

Long cravat (these were tied in bows at the side) scarf of lightweight, stiff silk, hand embroidered with oriental motifs. Label: 'Le Noeud de Paris'. **£20 / $33.** (*See Plate 9.*)

UMBRELLAS

The umbrella was the update of the Edwardian parasol – slim, elegantly furled, tall-handled umbrellas that stepped out alongside the high heels.

I have got two or three from this period, but my favourite is terracotta shading to deep cream with a fancy wood and plastic handle. On opening, it become a charming Chinese pagoda shape. About £10/$17 upwards depending on condition. And there's another one in the same shape with splodgey blue spots all over it. Very 'Singing in the Rain' looking.

A CONTROLLING 'FOUNDATION GARMENT'. A long-line *corselette* made from peach satin and powder net with underwired bust cups, six cased plastic spirals and six suspenders. Decorated with peach lace and pink velvet ribbon. Label: 'Made in France Expressly for Saks 5th Avenue'. £20/$33 upwards depending on condition and attractiveness.

HORROCKS

Technicolour films, new fabrics and washing-machines brought subtle colours into fashion that at one time would have been considered impractical. Horrocks, originally cotton cloth manufacturers, have a special place in the annals of ready-to-wear. In the 1860s, they seamed up some of the first, over-the-counter underwear. A hundred years later, they found themselves in considerable favour when Princess Margaret took some of their pretty cotton dresses on her honeymoon. Certainly the charming, colourful prints and easy-to-wear styles suited the effervescent years of the decade and make having a Horrocks – or similar – a must in any collection. Dresses are usually in good condition, although they were used summer after summer. The bug-bear of this period is the unalterable fact that from 1955 to 1960 the skirt length began to creep up, and sometimes the hems have been lopped, altering the balance of the dress. But women usually still had a 'waste not, want not' attitude and would painstakingly turn up rather than cut off a hem.

One of the popular 'wide' looks for the 1950s was the cotton dress. Usually this

A CIRCULAR-SKIRTED, SLEEVELESS, 'ballerina'-length summer dance dress in a crisp glazed cotton made by 'Horrockses'. This is a vivid, floribunda of a dress, a riot of big splodges in pinks, mauves, blues and greens. It's a size 16 and the lovely, happy lady who gave it to me must have looked like a French Impressionist's garden in full bloom. Missing a belt. About 1955. **£40-60/$66-100**. (*See Plate 9.*)

was a simple, close-fitting top to offset the full skirt.

A SLIM, MID-CALF, AFTERNOON DRESS made from a heavy, woven cream linen embroidered with sporadic swirls in navy braid. Fully lined, with a boat neckline, cap sleeves, inset half-sash that ties at hip level. With it a plain, matching 'swing' coat with large pockets and three-quarter 'bell' sleeves. It is such a beautiful, classic *ensemble* – you could wear it now without shame. It was worn with navy accessories, of course! Label: 'Elca Model'. 1952-54. **£60/$100**.

A TWO-PIECE, SHORT-SLEEVED TOP and full skirt, homemade from very heavy unbleached linen. The material design was executed by the artist who wore it – a repeating stencil in sage and maroon of Regency stripes and 'miniatures' tied up with ribbon. It is incredible. About 1950. **£60/$100**.

A NOTHER SHORT COCKTAIL cum dance dress made from a stiff nylon net in a pine green colour, with a bronze taffeta lining. The close-fitting, boned bodice has net ruched across the bust and stitched to the wide shoulder straps. The skirt is crisply, durably, sun-ray pleated and the dress fastens with a metal zip at the back. Label: 'Susan Small' (a well-regarded, ready-to-wear label of the decade). It's a charming dress. Fair condition. About 1952. **£45/$75**.

B LACK AND CLEAR LUCITE envelope evening bag with *diamanté* decoration to corner. About 1955. **£60/$100**. And a black and gold casket Lucite handbag with one handle and gold finials. 1950-55. **£100-120/$165-200**. (*See Plate 1.*)

S MALL, BRIGHT GOLD, metal mesh evening bag with rounded gilt metal frame with snaps and wrist loop of finer mesh. Lined with gold-coloured silk, the whole purse is strong and well made. Label: 'Whiting Davies Co. Mesh Bags. Made in U.S.A.' Whiting Davies is the big name in mesh. Founded as a jewellery firm in the 1870s, it became known for its fine quality purses. About 1950. **£22/$36**.

1920s purses are very delicate, often painted. The later ones in the 1950s and 1960s have a flat, silky finish and are dazzling.

CLOSE-FITTING TURBAN HAT in ocelot printed wool jersey. Label: 'Paulette'. 2nd Label: 'Harrods'. Paulette, a French milliner, worked throughout the War and was famous for her jersey turbans. About 1955. **£30/$50.**

This dress is worn by the floosy dummy who loiters in the darker regions of the vicarage.

SLEEVELESS, FIGURE-HUGGING dress, to the knee, in a rough-textured needlecord, printed like leopard skin. There are two slant pockets at the hips, a hefty metal zip at the side and it's worn with wide, black plastic belt. It's big

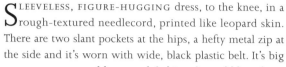

and busty and (whisper) would have been considered very tarty in its day, but it's interesting to see this 'animal' look, which has gone in and out of fashion many times, enjoying a prowl in the Fifties. No label (cut out). About **£15/$25** – more when these prints are in fashion.

ACCESSORIES

Rock 'n' rollers wore wide elastic belts and little white ankle socks *over* their seamed, tan stockings and, on their feet, flat black pumps. The most vivid memory is their hair – curly pony-tails, *à la* Brigitte Bardot, tied up with transparent nylon scarves, the ends flying as they twirled. Believe me, nylon scarves were a cult thing of the 1950s; they were a bit down market ('Pure Woolworth's' as my mother would have said), but they were cheerful and attractive. It was nice to have something to soften a neckline or fuss up a frock, and, usually, aunties wore them to keep 'perms' undisturbed on a breezy day. I have some lovely examples in bright blue, red, yellow, lime green, shocking pink with a pattern of roses, pale pink with Lurex threads

running through, pale blue with pinky mauve edges – all sorts. I love them.

In fact, to be well turned-out, each dress or suit in the 1950s had its own hat, shoes, bag, maybe a scarf, let alone beads and brooch – and gloves. All these could 'bring up' an outfit. Often accessories were a matching colour (or near). Working-class women wanted to look like the middle classes or the Royal family. In summer, it was easier – cotton dresses usually went with white accessories – but spring, autumn and winter could mean whole sets of separate items.

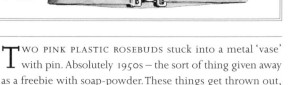

TWO PINK PLASTIC ROSEBUDS stuck into a metal 'vase' with pin. Absolutely 1950s – the sort of thing given away as a freebie with soap-powder. These things get thrown out, so are fun to find. **50p/80 cents.** (*See illustration above.*)

Y ELLOW PLASTIC HANDBAG, shaped like a sandcastle, with Lucite lid decorated with anemones. Catch missing. About 1950. £28/$46. *(See front jacket illustration.)*

GLOVES

Most of all, gloves were the sartorial success of the 1950s. Gloves, those trademarks of gentility, now covered the hands of the masses as well as those above stairs. Stretch fabrics ousted fine leathers, cotton jersey and nylon (we liked sheer nylon for brides) replaced the doe skin and silk of former days. All ladies' wear shops sold gloves, in all colours and patterns (spots were very popular) – short 'bracelet' and 'formal' long. Big department stores were still considered glove specialists and sold fine, imported French gloves alongside cotton ones. They had once been lumped in with haberdashery but now needed counters to themselves. Pairs of gloves from the 1950s onwards are interesting, varied and cheap to buy. The great name to look for is Dents.

O NCE UPON A TIME, I went to learn shorthand and typing at a school in London, and there were girls there who really danced rock 'n' roll a treat, earnestly practising steps in the lunch hour (with no music – other girls stood round humming 'Singing the Blues', etc., and clapping the beat). I remember they wore a sort of uniform (vaguely Teddy Girl) - white blouses with magyar sleeves (cooler) and stand up 'New Elizabethan' collars, often with a black velvet ribbon choker, and black circular skirts made from shiny acetate material, like one lined in red with side button fastening. About 1955. £15-20/$25-33.

V ERY SMART WHITE COTTON blouse with three-quarter sleeves, wide cuffs and stand-up wing collar. Fastened with dark grey pearl buttons. Label: 'Richard Lynn Ltd. London'. £12/$20. *(See Plate 9.)*

H ALF-HAT MADE FROM sprays of lily of the valley (Dior's favourite flower). About 1950. £20-25/$33-40. *(See Plate 14.)*

T RIANGULAR-SHAPED, GREY-GREEN plastic handbag with coiled gilt ring handle, zip fastening at one side and gilt glove-clip attached. About 1955. £12/$20.

HANDBAGS

The handbags here are rather expensive, so look out for all sorts of other plastic and vinyl bags from the 1950s. The United States did lots in clear vinyl with flowers, shells and old coins 'framed' beneath. In this country, the high street, 'fashion' bag was very popular and there are hundreds, thousands to be found everywhere, at car boot sales, charity shops and jumble sales.

Fine quality leather bags still came from either big jewellers (if they sold cutlery, they likely sold frame bags – metal is the connection), department stores or specialist luggage shops. There's a lovely choice for collectors. Prices vary from £10/$17 to a few hundred, depending on condition and what name is on the label. I never worry about condition if it's an interesting example. You expect a good leather handbag to have been well used and cared for.

SMALL, BROWNY FAWN LEATHER frame bag with snap clasp and self-handle. Inside it still has the original tissue paper and a swing label: 'This handbag is fully guaranteed by Spiers. Congratulations on your choice (3 months)'. And, best of all, the original bill: 'Mushroom leather H/bag £1-4-0d. 21/7/59'. **£15/$25.**

DUMPY LITTLE FRAME BAG like a loaf, covered in a pretty floral 'upholstery' material with self-loop handle and gilt snap. Inside it had a silver confetti horseshoe, a tiny screw pot of 'Laleek' (cream for your eyelashes) and a 'Dinkie' wave-gripper. About 1950. **£7/$12.**

I'm putting in lots of bags because, like shoes, bags give you an instant picture of how fashion developed in a decade.

HARD PLASTIC (Americans call it Lucite) casket bag. I have half a dozen in the collection (one has matching strappy sandals, marked 'Citations, USA'), but the bag that intrigues me most is a deep amber colour, 7 × 4 inches, with 2 handles and 4 screw-in ball feet. The whole bag is engraved like cut-glass and is fairly heavy. Label on hinged lid: 'Original Rialto. N.Y.' About 1950. **£75/$122 upwards.**

CLEAR, RECTANGULAR Lucite bag (7 × 4 inches), with 'engraved' lid, horse-shoe handle and gilt clasp. No maker's label. About 1950. **£70/$115 upwards.**

A SMALL 'COCKTAIL' BAG with a handle (to dangle on your wrist whilst handling a glass, cigarette, sausage on a stick, etc.), metal framed, box shape (there were still lots of flat-bottomed handbags that 'stood' when put down). This one is made from black satin covered with brightly painted flowers, also on the frame and handle, and is then intricately overlaid with tiny glass beads in similar colours. At a quick glance, it looks like petit point (lots of those around in the 50s and 60s, beautifully embroidered in France or Austria), but it must have been even harder to do. All the hinges and snaps are gilt and it has a silk interior with purse and other sections. It's an amazing piece. Label: 'Waldybag. Made in England'. About 1950. £55/$90. (See Plate 1.)

It was only a week or two ago that I realized this bag glowed in the dark because its beads are luminous.

HATS

And cocktails makes me think of hats. It was still the thing to wear a *small*, witty hat perched on top of the perm to go to an early evening party, before going on to the theatre. Satin, velvet, net, feathers, sparkle, head-gripping shapes – these are the things to look for in collectable hats of the 1950s. All the best milliners did them: Simone Mirman, Freddie Fox, Aage Thaarap, Otto Lucas – to name but four posh ones – but there are dozens of desirable labels out there. £10/$17 to *much more, depending. (See Plate 14)*

S WEET 'JULIET' CAP made from fawn silk with blown glass beads – they're ripening red-currants or something. Also a tiny red straw 'beany' which drips Morello cherries. American. 1950-55. About £20/$33 each.

A N EVENING PURSE or 'Party Case'. *Very* heavy, curved metal case, hinged in two halves and enamelled in light green, pink and gold, depicting Persian warriors and animals. Fine mesh handle with central medallion. The interior is lined in pink satin with separate cases for powder, hairpins, lipstick, purse and comb. Kept in original grey felt cover. Label: 'Stratton'. 1953. £50-60/$82-100.

A DAINTY, LADYLIKE, FRAME BAG made from soft, pale brown fur with a fawn leather handle. It's an 'afternoon' bag, a bit of a novelty and something to talk about when you went out to tea. You bet – because the fur is Kangaroo and it's marked 'Present from Kangaroo Traders, Australia'. Actually, it's ghastly – but different. About 1955. £15/$25.

A BLACK SATIN, SNAP-FRAME evening bag with handle, square shape, 8 × 6 inches, with screen-printed reproduction of eighteenth-century romantic pastoral painting on front and back. Inside is a separate printed purse and, delightful, a powder compact, also silk lidded, with a picture of two cherubs. Very pretty (and much like the things Vivienne Westwood has designed during the 1990s). Not a label in sight but lovely condition. **£45/$75.**

F ITTED PALE BLUE/GREY striped nubbed tweed jacket for a tailored town suit with neat collar and lapels. It has a 4-button fastening (plain, toning) with two flap pockets and side button detail at hips. The distinctive Art Deco label is woven with a stylized Diana and hound: 'Matita. Goddess of Sport. London, Paris, New York. Made in England'. (*See illustration opposite.*) The jacket is typical of the 'unnoticed' but chic clothes that Matita specialized in. Started in the mid-1920s by Max Adler, it produced beautiful copies of simple, elegant French designs, including some of the first Chanel look-alikes, for middle-class women who could not afford originals. Other firms of this ilk were Jaeger, Cresta, Dereta and Dorville. About 1955. **£28/$46.**

R ARE SHIRT BLOUSE IN Hawaiian-style with amusing, topical design ad-vertising 3 great musicals of the 1950s – *My Fair Lady*, *West Side Story* and *Gigi* – in bright greens, yellows, shocking pink and black lettering. Label: 'Ann Dell. SportsWear'. (Probably American.) About 1958. **£50-60/$82-100.**

C LASSIC TWO-PIECE in fine woven terracotta wool, comprising an unlined, easy-fitting jacket, decorated with self-embroidered cut-work and a knee-length skirt with pleats front and back. Superbly made from excellent cloth. Label: 'Mori Sport'. Hanae Mori, born in 1926, is one of the first Japanese couturiers (there are so many) to find international fame. She opened her first shop in Shinjuku and, in 1955, another in Tokyo, and found huge success in both America and France. This is a rare example of her early work. About 1955. **£30/$50 upwards.**

A(FULL) BOX OF 'Coty' face powder – the orangey 'Powder Puff' box (designed by René Lalique) is very distinctive, you'd know it immediately – in a shade called 'Continentale', still smelling of *Muguet de Bois*. **£4/$7.**

ATWO-INCH GILT METAL lipstick container with look-ing-glass that shoots up and nearly knocks your teeth out. Stamped 'Stratton' (the name everyone remembers for compacts). Inside is a Helena Rubenstein lipstick. **£3/$5.**

THREE-INCH WALLET with stud fastening in pearlized pink plastic (say that after two glasses of sherry), inside which is a looking-glass and a wad of Number Seven lip tissues. Slotted along the edge is a squat case still containing a pink bullet called 'Coral Spice'. In the 1950s (and 1960s), a name like that held images of the sun and fun you were saving up for on your holiday, be it at Butlins or Benidorm **50p/80 cents.**

AWHITE PLASTIC SHELL that at one time contained a little dark blue bottle of 'Evening in Paris'. (Local cinemas reeked of this scent.) **50p/80 cents.**

CREAM 'LUXON' HIDE beauty case (think musical jew-ellery boxes with revolving ballerinas) with two sen-sible handles, opening to reveal crimson Rayon and a vast array of plastic bottles and pots. These cases were popular for holiday travel, but the glamorous image is of fashion model girls who used to carry their make-up, shoes, etc. around from salon to salon in them. Stamped inside: 'Maylor. London'. About 1954. **£15/$25.**

Just a moment ago, I tripped over a big carrier bag in the Costume Room (Ollie dropped his beastly ball in it) which houses this ultimate accessory for the 1950s.

TYPICAL OF THE 1950S, a four-stranded, imitation, grad-uated pearl necklace with decorative paste clasp. **£20/$33.** (*See Plate 8.*)

A THREE-STRAND BEAD necklace in pink, blue and green frosted glass that has large clasp with inset rhinestones, the kitsch glitz of the decade. Such strands of beads remained popular with 'mature' ladies from the mid-1950s to the 1970s. There are thousands of them around and I bet someone in your family has some. (*See Plate 9.*)

S IMPLE NECKLET OF *diamanté* drops with a chrome metal link backing. £10/\$17. (*See Plate 9.*)

JEWELLERY

Lots of 1950s sparkle is still around – collars, cuffs, belts and brooches – real and ever so not. Look out for 'Poppet' snap-together beads and bracelets and brooches made of woven plastic thread in bright colours. Earrings came in lots of different styles, but mostly clusters or gilt flower or leaf shapes, sometimes curving 'up' the ear (we were terribly in love with chief swan Margot Fonteyn). But the outstanding favourites were classic pearls, clips or screw ons. These you'll find from **20p/30cents to £20,000/ \$33,000.**

F LOWER BROOCHES of every kind were popular, pretty and either real or costume. A biggish 'branch' with safety swivel (these came in during the late 1940s to 1950s) on pin, painted gold with 2 black stones that look like aubergines, but I don't think they're meant to be. Marked: 'Jewelcraft'. Canadian. Cheap, not cheerful, but typical. £2-3/\$3-5.

A N OVAL BROOCH with coloured 'everlasting' flowers set under a Perspex dome. £10/\$17. A clear, facet-edged Lucite brooch with four pink and white flowers. £3/\$5. Round Lucite brooch with a frilly edge showing a crinolined lady with parasol. About 1950. £10/\$17.

A LADY'S CIGARETTE CASE with felt cover. Very slim and made from gilt with scrolled edge and black enamelled top with red rose in the centre. Containing three 'Passing Cloud' cocktail cigarettes. It was considered sophisticated to carry cigarettes even if you didn't smoke. Such was the way of the world. Made by Stratton. £10-12/\$17-20.

O NE-INCH LIMOGES china picture of two Arcadian lovers in a gilt surround, marked 'Fragonard', and likely copied from one of his paintings. £10/\$17. Royal Crown, done in gilt and gaudy pastes. **£5/$8.** Gilt charm bracelet dangling with Royal crown and 'All the Queen's Men'. **50p-£4/80 cents -$7.**

Two-inch white china plaque showing the young Elizabeth II in the centre of a gold, red and blue circle. Stamped on pin, which has elaborate safety catch: 'Coal-port. Made in England'. 1953. **£10-20/$17-33.**

Two-inch powder compact (with case) with purple enamelled top and Royal coat-of-arms, inscribed 1953 with a leter 'E' picked out in red pastes. Label: 'Vogue Vanities'. **£12-15/$20-25.**

Four-inch stiletto winkle-picker-toed shoes in blue satin. Size 4. Italian. 1958-60. **£25/$40.** (*See Plate 9.*)

Mid-calf, sleeveless, sheath cocktail dress in a fancy material made from white net, completely covered in scrolls of ruched white nylon braid and stitched scrunchy plastic tape that glitters like ice. The wide neckline and front bodice have large crystal drops sewn in a 'v' to the waist. Back fastens with long zip. Label: 'Margaret Paynton. London'. About 1955. **£60-70/$100-115.** (*See Plate 9.*)

CORONATION SOUVENIRS

Anything to do with the Coronation (or any Royal occasion) is always worth collecting. I have scarves commemorating this event and a dance dress and stole that was dress-maker made in cream Rayon satin and then painstakingly hand embroidered with all the UK emblems and worn to a regimental do on Coronation night. Worth **£80-100/$132-165 (more in an anniversary year).**

Black plastic shoe bag with zip and handle, containing black and gold brocade dance shoes with 'looped material' toes and 3-inch heels. Label: 'Flickerstrap by Clarks'. This was still a decade when, if you didn't have a car (and lots of people didn't) and went to a dance via public transport or Shanks's pony, you changed your shoes when you got there. Such shoes twinkled the night away before they caught the NO. 47 home. Good condition. **£15/$25.**

FILMY SILK SCARF printed with black and white poodles. Poodles were the dogs of the decade – look out for brooches, skirts, bags, etc., all displaying French poodle motifs. £2/$3.

A symphony of nylon. My dress-maker's dummy Moll is in it and positively twitching with excitement. It's every little girl's dream of a dressing-up dress.

FULL-SKIRTED, SIZE 10, 'Come Dancing' ballerina-length dress in shimmering white nylon with 'paint effect' bunches of pink and blue roses with emerald leaves and scattered rhinestones. It has a close-fitting bodice, fully boned, with pink net shoulder straps and matching layered petticoats. Fastens with pink metal zip at the back. No label. Professionally, strongly sewn: a tough but sensational dance dress. About 1955. £45-50/$75-82.

PAIR OF POWDER BLUE suede court shoes, decorated with small self-bow, with very pointy toes and 4-inch steel stiletto heels, called 'pin heels'. Entirely different in shape from those of the early 1950s, these fashion shoes were being imported from France and Italy by the end of the decade. Eventually, all the high street shops did pin heels. Label: 'Creatzioni Chanda di L'Invitta. Made in Italy'. Very good condition and very sexy. 1958-60. £25-30/$40-50.

EXTREMELY SMART, GREY and white check, seersucker cotton coat-dress. Double-breasted style with large collar, three-quarter length sleeves, wide skirt with flapped, hip pockets and half-belt, fastened with large, pearl grey buttons. Unworn. Label: 'Slimuette'. Swing label still attached: 'An entrance is *made* in Slimuette'. This is such an interesting example of the high street New Look. I've had this outfit for years but it's still fresh and elegant. About 1952. £60-70/$100-115.

SKY BLUE NYLON WAIST petticoat decorated with bands of deep white nylon lace. Label: 'Etam. Size M'. About 1955. £5-10/$8-17.

A WASPIE SUSPENDER BELT in pale blue satin, an Edwardian-inspired clincher with incredibly strong elastane inserts (talk about 'power' elastic), long ruffled suspenders and a flange of hooks and eyes. No label. About 1950. £25-30/$40-50.

DEEP ROSE PINK LACE bikini briefs (but not teeny like they are now). Label: 'St Michael. Lingerie'.

All these knickers from the 1950s can be found for a few pounds, or even pence, at jumble and boot sales.

NAVY BLUE, WHITE SPOTTED nylon briefs with a little pink rose on the elastic waist. Label: 'St Michael. Nylon'. 2nd Label: 'This garment should be washed separately'.

PALE PINK NYLON BRIEFS, frilled over the bottom like babies' knickers with elasticated waist and legs. Label: 'Kayser'. Swing label still attached: 'This Size is W. Price 12/11d. Shade P. Pink. Made in the Republic of Ireland'.

ANOTHER PAIR IN PALE GREEN, pleated nylon and lace, with tiny skirt over attached briefs. Very pretty. Label: 'St. Michael. Lingerie'.

PAIR OF BLACK, 15-DENIER, seamed nylon stockings. Label: 'Plaza Fully Fashioned'. £3-5/$5-8.

A SLIP AND 'PANTIES' SET in pale pink nylon, trimmed with a white 'flocked' variety (love it) and bows. Label: 'Kayser –Tailored nylon jersey'. Now, this is a bit up-market, but nylon was considered as an attractive, easy care alternative to silk or Rayon in its early, high street years. £25-30/$40-50.

These undies are in good condition. Surprisingly, sets can be fairly pricey since nice nylon things get harder to find.

A SMALL, WHITE PLASTIC BOX with lift-up lid containing a pair of unworn, 'Carefree' (seamless) nylon stockings. The trade card included says 'Guaranteed Not to Snag – As Demonstrated on T.V. Carefree will outlast 9 pairs of ordinary nylons, will not ladder easily and are therefore wonderfully economical.' £6-8/$10-13. Imitation leather *pochette* for keeping nylons safe and ladder-free. About 1955. £5/$8.

FULL, STIFF, 'PAPER' NYLON (you put sugar in the final rinse to keep it crackly), elasticated waist petticoat overlaid with puffs of sheer pink and net. For evening, under a full skirt, you wore two or three of these stiff creations, often snagging the precious nylon stockings. Label: 'Styled by Chaslyn regd.' 1958-60. **£20/$33 (you can find them at all prices, but the elaborate ones are more expensive).**

STRAPLESS, LONG-LINE BRASSIÈRE in flesh pink, opaque nylon and power elastic. Lots of seaming and curvaceous ironwork to give oomph to the 36-inch bosom. Label: 'Lilees by Lily of France'. £20-25/$33-40.

BLOW-UP BRA

I've also got an inflatable bra from the 1950s. It's called 'Très Secret' (unfortunately, only one side works as the other seems to have developed a puncture). I also have some of those whirlpool-stitched, pointed cones in the collection. These are treasures from the Golden Age of Bras and sadly not often stumbled upon.

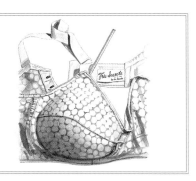

Thousands of schoolgirls, including me, wore pairs similar to this – usually in a dark colour (with linings) such as navy, maroon, bottle green – under a matching, pleated, gym-slip.

PAIR OF DARK BROWN, pure wool, 'shrink resisting' (this 'shrink' business was the bane of housewives), jersey lock-knit school bloomers. Elasticated top and leg ends plus wide, double re-inforced gusset. Outside pocket on right (for your hanky or conkers, or something). Overall length, 18 inches. Label: 'Utility made by Chilprufe. CC41. Size 8.' Original card price tag: '15/6d'. Practical and dignified and something that women educationalists had struggled hard to introduce at the end of the nineteenth century. Believe it or not, bloomers like these are lusted after in all corners of the globe; I could name my price for these evocative items! About 1950.

There would also be a wide elastic belt and, glory, a plastic, bucket-shaped shoulder bag with a bright pink 'Gala' lipstick inside.

WHAT WE REALLY WANTED to get into was this bright green circular skirt made from felt with hip pockets edged with black bobble fringe. £40/$66. (See Plate 9.) Worn with black, silky, low-necked, cap-sleeved sweater, decorated with white embroidery and rhinestone flowers. Label: 'Thorn Craft Knitwear London'. £20/$33.

A TINY 'G'-STRING, made of sheer white nylon with a pussycat's face embroidered in black on the front panel. Label has been washed out, but definitely not a high street item. The shop that sold the best 'naughties' in London in my youth was Weiss in Shaftesbury Avenue, London. **£3 / $5.**

A LONG-SKIRTED HOUSECOAT made from opaque pink, easy-care nylon, printed with large cabbage roses in deep blue, maroon and white. It has pockets and a self-sash. Lots of women seemed to possess one of these garments, the intermediary between getting properly dressed and being up and 'seeing to things' around the house before you did so. It was one up on the dressing-gown and curlers look and you didn't frighten the gas-man. Label: 'A Su-Ray model. 100% nylon'. About 1953. **£25 / $40.**

H ERE'S GRACE KELLY, a heavy, white cotton dress with full skirt and shoulder straps, decorated with blue gimp thread and elaborate floral design in white beads and pale blue sequins. A summer dance/cocktail dress, worn with a swing Duster Coat (originally a throw-on to keep the clothes clean when travelling in an open motor car) with huge shawl collar and three-quarter length sleeves in matching, blue ribbed cotton. Absolutely typical of a dressy outfit in about 1955. Very well made. Label: '*Modele* Shandel. London W.1.' **£25 / $40 upwards.** (*See Plate 9.*)

FIFTIES LOOKS

The other look the young favoured was modern Chinese, a straight, slit-up-the-side, high-necked *cheongsam*-Suzy Wong look. This style (revived as I write) became popular after the successful staging of the musical *Tea-House of the August Moon*. Watch out for dressy clothes made in beautiful Chinese brocades from this period.

Another mid-1950s fashion was 'Sloppy Joe' Italian knits in bright colours, with tapering, just above the ankle, trousers called Pedal Pushers. They were called Capri Pants in the 1960s and 1970s. Not many of these are still around, but you may be lucky.

A SHORT-SLEEVED, SUMMER day dress of charcoal grey cotton printed in large, bold, bright colours of orange, lemon and green, featuring an Egyptian scene. The dress is slightly 'A' line (the next Dior inspiration, in 1953) with lower waist and full skirt, which includes a stiffened underskirt, springing from hip yoke. It is closed at the back by a long, heavy zip with 'Pilot' on the tag. Label: 'Sally Slade of Regent Street'. It's the sort of dress thousands of women bought who were beginning not to sew their own. About 1954. **£20-30/$33-50.**

C & A did brilliant, quick-off-the-mark, 'Paris to Peckham' clothes in the 1950s and 1960s.

ANOTHER 'A'-LINE DRESS. Plain pink waxed cotton, sleeveless with narrow shoulder straps, self-belted at a natural waist, long bodiced but with the attached tarlatan (stiffened muslin) petticoat pushing out the skirt at the hip. A charming dress. No label but I know it was bought by the original owner at the Marble Arch branch of C & A Modes in about 1956 and she probably paid £3 or £4. **£20-30/$33-50.**

QUITE LARGE HANDBAG (they got bigger and bigger to balance the shorter skirts by the end of the decade). 14 × 8 inches, a snap-frame, traditional bag with single handle. Stone-coloured plastic to look like leather with panel of hand-stitched wool tapestry showing two roses in shades of pink and heliotrope. Interior lined in 'suedette'. A mix of stuffs, like upholstery fabric, tapestry, or Swiss embroidered linen with leather, was popular for bags and shoes. No label. Good condition. About 1959. **£28/$46.**

EVENING DRESSES

The grandeur of evening dress was re-established for middle and upper ranks of society in the 1950s. All the great dress designers were doing extravagant, beautiful clothes for after dark. In this country, led by Norman Hartnell (he did the Royal ladies repeatedly proud), we strove to take on all the pomp and circumstance of big occasion dressing. Echoing the opulence of Victorian high life, the ball-gown was once more in a class of its own.

A MODEL OF IT'S DAY IS A heavy, strapless, tight-bodiced and close-boned dress made from ruby red twilled silk, the top completely plain, with large box pleats sweeping down to appliquéd lace flowers and cream-coloured embroidery with a final flourish of 6-inch frilling of scalloped organdy. All this is supported by a retinue of fixed net petticoats and a separate, plastic-boned 'hoop'. It's all very Scarlett O'Hara. To fasten, two fine metal zips to do up the back – one for the lining, one for the outer bodice. Splendidly made, lots of hand finish. Label: 'Harald. 39a Curzon Street, London'. 1950-55. **£100-150/$165-248.**

ANOTHER GRAND, FULL-LENGTH ball-gown with lots of built-in petticoats of ice blue ribbed silk, the bell-shaped skirt cut in smooth panels that flow and widen from the figure-hugging, beaded and sequinned bodice. This is stiff with interior plastic boning, all wonderfully and strongly sewn. Romantic and classy. Label: 'Jean Allen'. 1951 (Festival of Britain year). **£100/$165 upwards.** (See Plate 8.)

TWIN-SETS

Don't forget about twin-sets, will you? The Fifties isn't done until you've got a twin-set in your collection. Marks and Spencer, Littlewoods, British Home Stores – they all did them. Hurry, you have to get to them before all those voracious Agatha Christie period drama wardrobe people beat you to it. **£10/$17** in nice condition and more if the look is in fashion.

TRADITIONAL WEDDING DRESS in 'pretend' (acetate) ivory satin brocade, the style reminscent of the Royal Tudors. Long sleeves with points over the hands, sweetheart neckline, stiffened underskirt. With original embroidered net veil and wax and diamanté head-dress. **£80/$132.**

PAIR OF SILVER LEATHER stiletto-heeled evening shoes with narrow pointed toes. Label: 'Lilley & Skinner Starlight Room'. 1958-60. **£12-15/$20-25.** (See Plate 8.)

ONE-PIECE BATHING-SUIT in white cotton printed with vibrant pink rose buds. Button on, halter neck with shirred elastic back (which would have left a trellis pattern on her bottom). The suit has two cased plastic 'Flexi' bones over bosom. No label, but lots of erstwhile corsetry firms dived into swimwear after the War. 1956-58. **£25/$40.**

BUCKET-SHAPED beach bag in navy blue with white spots and shoulder strap. **£6/$10.** Pair of black patent, point-toed, needle-thin stilettos, trimmed with black and white spotted bow. Label: 'Rayne'. Fair condition. **£18-20/$30-33.** (See also Plate 9.)

A LIME GREEN AND WHITE sun-suit with shirred elastic 'body' and a short, attached circular skirt. 1956-58. £25-30 / $40-50.

P AIR OF POINTED, stiletto-heeled shoes made from a cream corded fabric sprigged with tiny flowers. Label: 'Peerless'. About 1955. £30 / $50. (See Plate 7.)

U NUSUAL PINK PLASTIC sun-glasses, no glass lenses but horizontal slats of white plastic, like fan shutters, fixed across the eyepieces. British patent. £15 / $25 upwards.

This is quite an out-fit, but was chosen to be practical: many brides chose dresses that they could use as dance frocks afterwards, but few actually did without having them dyed.

M ADE-TO-MEASURE BRIDAL ARRAY. A beautifully tailored, 2-piece dress of plain, ivory ribbed silk with tiny waist, skirt cut in flaring panels (yards of it), strapless boned bodice and exterior quilted panels at the hips sewn with tiny pearls. Worn over the top, a tight-fitting 'mess' jacket with padded shoulders, quilted cuffs and stand-up collar, again decorated with pearls. 33 self-covered buttons and loops fasten the front of the jacket. A fitted net petticoat is worn underneath and the bride wore a plain tulle veil and wax orange blossom head-dress. Label: 'Michel (Mayfair) Ltd. 50a Curzon Street, w1. Designed by Michael Bronze'. 1952. £70-80 / $115-132.

M Y FAVOURITE HAT from the 1950s in the collection is this tiny boater, very Gigi, made from black and gold striped satin, the small brim padded to a small rolled shape and decorated with a plain black petersham ribbon with stiffened bow at back and small swathe of veiling in front. No label. About 1955. £20 / $33. (See Plate 14.)

T HE LITTLE BLACK DRESS. This was given electric shock treatment by Givenchy's dressing of the film star Audrey Hepburn. The ubiquitous, simple black dress, loved in the 1920s and 1930s, once more became a trusted friend to elegant, fashion-conscious women. It is at its classical best made from a fine woollen cloth, a material that has found favour with most great designers in the last hundred years.

The dress I was given had belonged to a beautiful, aristocratic lady – and its restrained charms reflect this. It's difficult to describe because the cut is so subtle. Basically, it's a narrow (weeny) sheath, in fine wool, a sleeveless tunic with separate, back panel attached at the neck and just caught at the waist in a sort of pouch. This hides the long, fine metal zip that closes the back. The dress is plain apart from a slight asymetrical 'drag' to the front and a piece of inch-wide black velvet ribbon that curves, diagonally, bust to hip, from right to left, ending in small, flat bows at the back. Lined throughout, professionally hand finished, with all the strength and confidence of a *couture* workroom. Christian Dior died in 1957, and this dress is certainly influenced by him. It could be by Balenciaga or Givenchy. Late 1950s. **£65-80/$108-132.**

U NDERNEATH SHE MIGHT have a black nylon lace *petit basque* corselette with long suspenders made by 'Warners' and called a 'Merry Widow'. About 1955. **£15/$25.**

B ESPOKE (you could be measured and fitted in your own home by a trained corsetière) strapless bra – with a little suspender belt – made from black lace over flesh pink nylon, the bra fully boned with clinching panels of elastane at the sides. Label: 'Spencer, London and New York. Individually Designed Underwear'. **£15/$25.**

Lots of seductive 'black on pink' undies arrived by the late 1950s. Sexual encounters at the cinema (on screen) are the reason.

MEN'S UNDERWEAR 1950

T HESE ARE POSITIVELY next-to-nothing coverings compared to what has gone before. A pair of whiter-than-white briefs (well laundered over the years) with the famous 'Y'-front. Not a button in sight and the first 'designer' pants, with its name on the elasticated waistband. An American patent, the style was produced under license in this country from 1938. This pair is cotton mesh – 'Celnet' – and looks like any other old 'Y'-front you've ever seen. Initially it was a success with young men, but not with old dads, unless they happened to be jockeys. But in the end their women thought these were better – and easier to wash. Label: 'Y-Front regd. Made in Scotland by Lyle & Scott'. About 1955. **10p/16 cents.**

THE 1960S BOOTS, BIBA AND BOUTIQUES

I expect fashion history will present the 1960s as ten years teeming with exotic young women dressed in tiny mini-skirts and John Lennon caps. Like other romantic costume plots, this version has been selected as the only look worth considering in the 1960s. As it happens, the Sixties had several moods and messages, only one of which concerned extremely short skirts. Fashion journalists then and since have written thousands of paragraphs about the underlying themes. One was about the advent of the contraceptive pill, which enabled women to have choice as to when they started their families, creating a new woman with a confident image of herself. Such a theory may be true, but the world had moved on and all I can do is to take an eager costume collector through the confusing maze of fashion trends that tends to be overwhelming by this decade.

What fashion clues will you look for to lead to treasures from the Swinging Sixies? Rule of thumb is simple, uncluttered lines, hems withdrawing up the leg, geometric patterns, bright colours and black and white Op Art. Accessories were getting similarly streamlined. Fancy-patterned tights and more eccentric fashion footwear were coming in, and hats were flowery at first, then simple helmet shapes, pull-ons and caps.

Jewellery was sculptural, bright, to be noticed. Look-alike materials – especially fur fabrics and imitation skins – were used. Underwear was lighter and there was less of it. Pop fashion exposure in magazines meant a youthful buyer's market, thus new shops and wacky young designers arrived catering exclusively for teens and twenties. Fashion had become an entertainment for the young, regardless of social background – their clothes showed a new democracy.

By about 1968, some free-thinkers had opted out of what they saw as an increasingly materialistic society. Western hippies wore clothes that were spontaneous, colourful, decorated and flowing – borrowed plumes from a mish-mash of Asian, African and Eastern cultures – and never before seen on quiet English streets.

But, thinking back, the 1960s started with most women still dressed in a look that had been designed ten years before. Soon, daughters certainly no longer wanted to look like their mothers – but the mothers yearned to look like their daughters, and did.

CLOTHES OF THE 1960S

I have tried to select an assortment of things that would have been worn by a range of women from different social spheres. But you will see that even with differences in making and cost, the prevailing fashion trends, now so widely advertised, begin to draw the classes together and it becomes harder to find a discriminating look between them. It is also marked how clothes, especially for the young, gain elements of theatricality and fantasy dressing-up by the late 1960s.

I'm starting with a jacket which straddles the late 1950s and the 1960s. Note how checks were in fashion.

SHORT, TO THE HIP, unfitted jacket in dark grey worsted with inch-square, fine white checks. It has an Eton collar and 2-inch 'hacking' vents at the back (that have a ton of tailor's weights enclosed). The front is decorated with 2 mock pockets and it fastens with 4 large fawn/grey buttons; lined with grey silk. No skirt (which might well have been plain grey). This shows some of the last links that persisted with a lady's tailor-made of the turn of the century. Label: 'Hardy Amies, 14 Savile Row, London. W.1.' Sir Hardy Amies is a superb tailor: born in 1909, he worked at Lachasse and Worth (London) Ltd., setting up his own House in 1946. He has dressed many Royal ladies and is known for elegant tailoring and sumptuous ball-gowns. About 1960. **£30-40/$50-66.**

A SUPER BLACK SILK 'beaver' fur cloche hat shaped like a deep, wide flower pot, trimmed with a black petersham bow. Label: 'Harvey'. About 1960. **£12/$20.**

BLACK, SHINY STRAW, Bretton sailor hat. Label: 'Claude Saint Cyr'. This milliner opened in Paris in 1937. Simplicity was her watchword, and she was possibly the most famous milliner in Paris from the 1940s to the 1960s. About 1960. **£30-40/$50-66.**

ELEGANT, STAND-UP black suede evening purse with hooped handle that you 'pinch' inward at the base to open the bag. No label. About 1960. **£20/$33.** (*See front jacket illustration.*)

L ARGE, SLOPING BRIMMED hat made from wired, sunset red silk organza, trimmed with large, full blown roses of that same colour. Label: 'Rayna model. Brompton Road'. 1960-62. **£5/$8 upwards.**

L ARGE BRIMMED HAT made from wired, black net with small gathers across the surface. Label: 'Christian Dior Boutique'. 1960-64. **£65/$108.**

A BELTED SHIFT DRESS with short, unfitted, button-through jacket in navy blue and white 'ink splodge' pattern. The jacket edges and pockets are bound with navy blue grosgrain ribbon and it has navy ball buttons. All lined in white silk with lots of hand finish. It is a nice, well-made, dull, safe outfit on a theme that was popular throughout the decade for 'slightly older' middle- and upper-class ladies, which meant anything from 35 to 90. Label: 'Hartnell. 26 Bruton Street'. About 1960. **£60-100/$100-165.**

NORMAN HARTNELL

Sir Norman Hartnell was born in 1901 and died in 1979. A Cambridge graduate who loved theatre design but was supposed to train as an architect, he instead opened his premises in Bruton Street with his sister (and a loan from his father) in 1923. In 1927, he showed his clothes to aclaim in Paris. Hartnell dressed the Royal ladies: he made the Queen's wedding dress and Coronation robes and is primarily remembered for his extravagant evening wear. He once said that he was 'partial to the jolly glitter of sequins'.

T HE FRENCH ARE ALWAYS ahead at this time, and Christian Dior opened his London off-the-peg 'boutique' in 1954. It sold clothes such as this narrow day outfit in shades of grey and white checked cashmere, with self-buttons, the lined coat with high-buttoned fluffy fur collar and fur cuffs. Underneath is a matching, sleeveless, high-waisted, lined tunic with a slight 'A'-line skirt, and both are worn to the knee. This outfit says what you need to know about the next stage of high fashion. Clothes begin to cover a smaller area of the body and the legs are exposed. These garments are beautifully cut, the material exactly right and there is lots of expert hand finish. Label: 'Christian Dior Boutique. London'. 1960. **£150/$248.**

Colour Plates

The clothes and accessories illustrated in the following colour
plates are described in detail in the text entries listed below.

Plate 8: 1950s Dress

Dress, p.121, second entry; shoes, p.121,
fourth entry; necklace; p.117, fourth entry.

Plate 9: 1950s

On dummies, left to right:
First dummy: dress, p.106, last entry; necklace,
p.114, first entry. Second dummy: dress and coat,
p.119, third entry. Third dummy: dress, p.115,
fifth entry; necklace, p.114, second entry.
Fourth dummy: suit, p.104, first entry; scarf,
p.105, last entry. Fifth dummy: blouse, p.109,
third entry; skirt, p.118, last entry.

On steps in foreground, left to right:
Blue stilettos, p.115, fourth entry; hat, p.105,
third entry; patent shoes, p.121, last entry;
black shoes, p.105, fourth entry; hat, p.105,
second entry.

Plate 10: 1960s

On dummies, left to right:
First dummy: dress, p.139, first entry; belt,
p.136, fifth entry. Second dummy: dress, p.140,
last entry. Third dummy: dress, p.138, second
entry; shoulder bag, p.145, fourth entry.
Fourth dummy: dress, p.132, fourth entry. Fifth
dummy: dress and coat, p.134, first entry.

On steps in foreground, left to right:
Two-tone shoes, p.129, third entry; gold
boots, p.131, third entry; red shoes, p.132,
first entry; white boots, p.131, fourth entry;
pink hat, p.133, last entry; spotted hat, p.139,
'Mary Quant' box; yellow shoes, p.145, third
entry; white handbag, p.131, first entry.

Plate 11: 1970s

On dummies, left to right:
First dummy: dress, p.154, third entry. Second
dummy: dress, p.151, first entry. Third dummy:
dress, p.136, seventh entry. Fourth dummy:
trouser suit, p.148, third entry; coat, p.148,
second entry. Fifth dummy: red jacket, p.152,
fourth entry; blue waistcoat, p.153, last entry;
trousers, p.150, first entry; shoulder bag,
p.155, last entry.

On steps in foreground, left to right:
Shoes, p.152, fifth entry; brown shoes, p.159,
second entry; white hat, p.150, second entry;
pile of shirts, p.149, second entry; platform
shoes, p.149, first entry; orange hat, p.158,
first entry.

Plate 12: 1980s

On dummies, left to right:
First dummy: suit, p.171, third entry. Second
dummy: wedding dress, p.162, second entry.
Third dummy: suit, p.171, second entry. Fourth
dummy: two-piece, p.166, sixth entry. Fifth
dummy: pin-stripe suit, p.166, fourth entry.

On steps in foreground, left to right:
Blue hat, p.171, last entry; white shoes, p.164,
fourth entry; black boots, p.164, third entry;
blue shoes, p.171, first entry.

Plate 13: 1990s

On dummies, left to right:
First dummy: suit, p.179, fourth entry. Second
dummy: dress, p.177, fourth entry. Third
dummy: jacket, p.177, second entry. Fourth
dummy: dress, p.184, first entry.

On steps in foreground, left to right:
Grey shoes, p.177, sixth entry; skeleton hat,
p.180, 'Hats' box; white hat, p.179, last entry;
shoes, p.177, sixth entry.

Plate 14: Hats

From top, left to right:
Small, dark navy straw boater decorated with
grey petersham band and a central cockade
of grey feathers in a silver buckle, from about
1895; straw hat, p.73, second entry; two
'fruit' cocktail hats, p.111, 'Hats' box; lily
of the valley, p.109, fourth entry; cream straw
boater with deep crown from about 1905;
ostrich feather, p.163, 'Weddings' box; black
and gold, p.122, last entry.

10

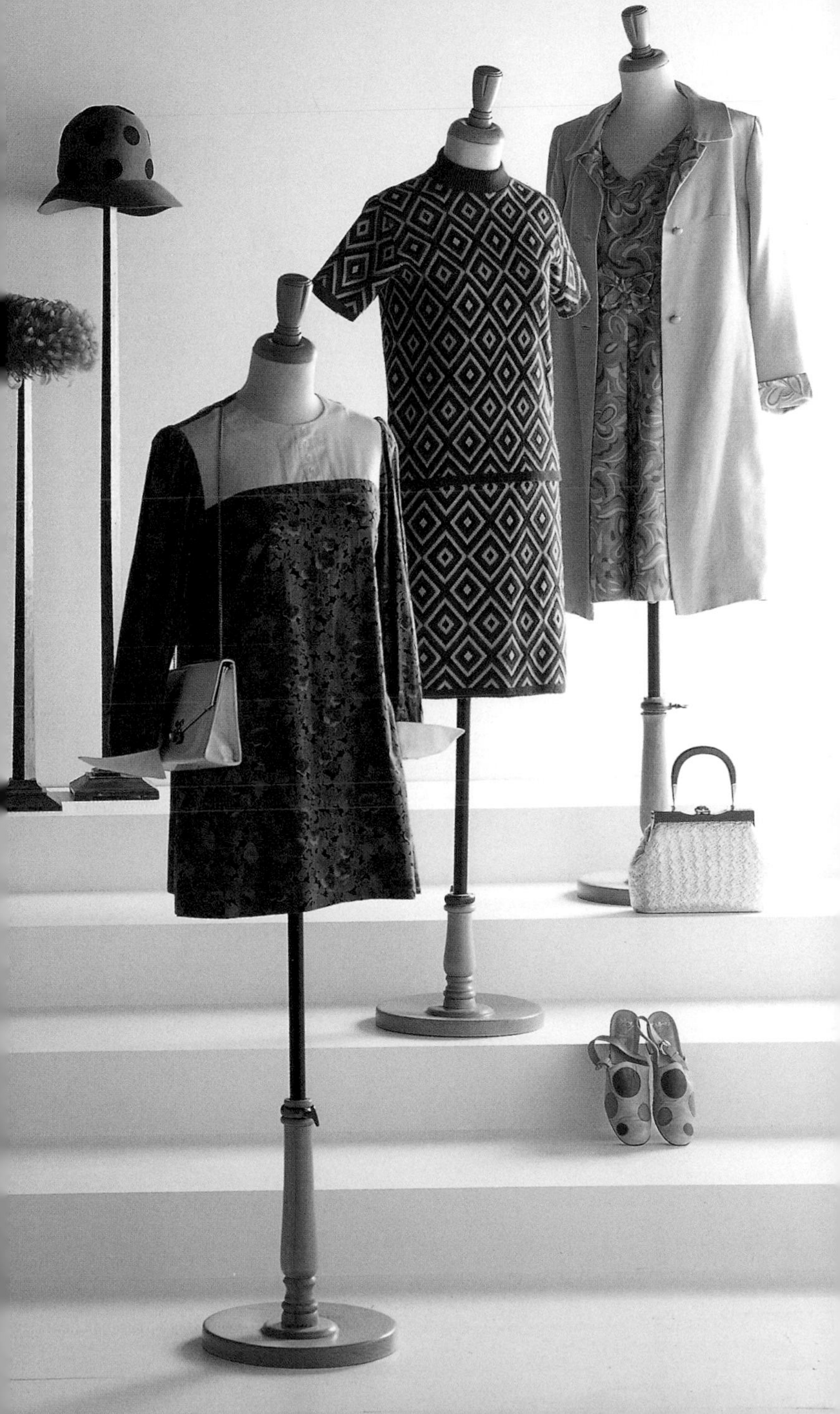

LACHASSE SUIT, SIZE 16, a cherry red and white hounds-tooth checked wool, clearly showing the 'boxy' look, an unfitted, waist-length jacket that was now fashionable. This has no fastenings, it just slips on, and there are a couple of decorative buttons at the shoulders and two recessed pockets. It is lined with white silk, as is the skirt, which is plain and to the knee. Label: 'Designed by Lachasse. London'. 1960-64. £2/$3 upwards.

PAIR OF VERY POINTY (winkle-picker) black calf shoes with suede trim and 3-inch pin heels. When I look at them, I know why I have ruined feet: there were no sloppily-shod feet in the early Sixties; women still responded to fashion dictators. Paris said strangle your toes, so we did. Label: 'Miss Rayne'. 1960-65. £25/$40.

PAIR OF BRIGHT GREEN, pointy-toed shoes with tiny Louis heels. Heels and trim in black. The dainty heels were designed to balance the shortening skirts. Label: 'Lordian Fashion Shoes. Made in France'. About 1961. £12/$20.

PAIR OF CLEAR AND BLACK vinyl shoes with small square toes, cut-out upper and one-inch Cuban heel. Label: 'Shoe-fayre. Jeune Parisienne'. About 1963. £30/$50. (*See Plate 10.*)

PAIR OF SPAGHETTI STRAPPED mules in pale blue, gold with pearl decorations and tiny, squat pedestal heels. Label: 'Dolcis. Cleopatra. Made in Italy'. About 1960. £3/$5.

PAIR OF BLACK SUEDE ankle boots, edged with black *guipure*, with zips (marked 'Flash'), pointy toes and small Louis heels. About 1960. £6.50/$11. Pair of opaque plastic galoshes. About 1960. 50p/80 cents.

PAIR OF RED LIZARD-SKIN shoes with pointy toes and tiny heels. Silk lined; label worn away. Possibly bespoke. About 1960. £20/$33. They went with a matching frame Mappin and Webb handbag. £25/$40. (*See Plate 1.*)

BRIGHT TURQUOISE BLUE cotton, full skirted (to the knee), petticoated, strapless sundress with self-buckle belt and stole with white fringed ends. The sort of summer holiday wear that thousands of girls chose in the early 1960s. Label: 'Victor Josselyn'. 1960-63. £35/$58.

LIGHT, FRAME SUMMER BAG (9 × 8 inches) with 2 handles, gilt buckle decoration and made from marble-effect yellow Corfam (synthetic coating over linen). The bag would drive you potty because the opening is so obscure – I sat for three minutes trying to do it (it works on a spring release clip that you can hardly see, an anti-burglary device). It's pretty nasty (posh places often do horrors), but a bit of Corfam is a collecting must. It probably went with a matching pair of shoes because it is made by Rayne, who usually did both. About 1964. £12-14/$20-24.

A CLUTCH BAG MADE OF hard plastic that looks like a rolled-up magazine. This one has a press-stud on a strap fastening and a laminated picture of children and a river and the title 'Journey' written in red. I have 4 of these, not one with a label, but they are made abroad, possibly in Italy or America. It's a witty idea. About 1966. £30-60/$50-100, depending on condition.

WOVEN, 'PEARLIZED' CREAM wicker basket cum handbag with two leather handles and wrap-over leather catch. Curved shape that opens in two halves and is cotton lined. Rather 'Costa del Sol'. About 1960. £3/$5.

BRIGHT RED SYNTHETIC leather, soft, loaf-shaped bag with amber plastic frame and red handle. Lined with cream Rayon. Label: 'Harmony. Made in England'. (I bet she had boots to match.) About 1968. £15/$25.

LIGHT, WHITE, PLAITED 'silk raffia' handbag, with wooden frame, gilt flip catch and single wooden handle. Covered with a clear plastic. Lined with white cotton with a zippered compartment. This is a high street version of the work of the Italian designer Emilio Gucci, who brought in bamboo handles in the 1960s. About 1966. **£20/$33.** (*See Plate 10.*)

BOOTS

I'll do some more bags in a moment, but now I must go back to feet.

By the mid-1960s, fashion boots were made for walking, dancing, posing and just saying 'Carnaby Street, here I come'. What you really want to find if possible is a pair of plain white boots with small chunky heels in either plastic or real leather. These were the cult by 1965 and have come to represent the whole decade. I haven't got a pair, but I show some boots of the same date, all with squarish toe-caps. They are all tightly-fitting, knee-high boots, and were even worn by fashion-conscious schoolgirls.

SHINY BLACK KNEE BOOTS with short, chunky plastic heels, leather feet and plastic coated material legs. Worn. Label: 'St. Michael'. About 1966. **£6/$10.**

PAIR OF GOLD LEATHER knee boots with flattish heels, instep zip and a small appliquéd butterfly decoration at the knee. These are lovely, and come complete with plastic boot-trees. About 1965. **£12-15/$20-25.** (*See Plate 10.*)

PAIR OF WHITE LEATHER knee boots with criss-cross cord lacings and inside leg zips. The 2½-inch heels are slightly flared. The outer sides are decorated with hand-painted exotic flowers. No label. Fine workmanship. Possibly Spanish or Italian. 1968-70. **£5/$8.** (*See Plates 7 and 10.*)

PAIR OF SYNTHETIC snake-skin knee boots with chunky heels. Very worn. Snake-skin was popular cladding; somewhere I've got a mini-coat that is a marvellous plastic snake. About 1966. **£5/$8.**

These shoes represent the little girl look of the late 1960s, characterized by such famous waifs as the model Twiggy.

Pair of red velvet, square-toed, seventeenth-century-looking evening shoes with squat gold leather heels and large, round gilt buckles. Label: 'K. Geiger, 53 New Bond Street'. 1969. £20-30/$33-50. (See Plates 7 and 10.) Pair of champagne gold evening shoes with square toes, sugar-cube heels and fine bar-straps. Label: 'Panama'. About 1966. £10-12/$17-20.

Short dance dress (to Twist in), to the knee, in ruby red satin brocade embroidered with gold thread. It has a boned bodice, two shoulder straps, a bow at the side waist and several internal net petticoats, including a feather-boned hooped one. In other words, it's a mini-crini. Label: 'Ricchi Michaels, Mayfair'. About 1960. £80-100/$132-165.

There's not much you can say about a Crimplene dress except that they were made in their thousands and lots of women loved them.

Straight, sleeveless crimplene dress in pale blue and white stripes. Very easy care. Dacron, Acilan, Courtell, Orlon and Dralon are all close cousins of Crimplene. Lots of British ladies had a white Orlon or Dycel cardigan to ward off the chills of a summer day – even when it was 86 degrees in the shade. Try as you may, you can't avoid having some ageing acrylics in a collection. 1960 onwards. £2/$3.

Machine-knitted, short-sleeved, short-skirted jumper suit in hot Italian colours – cerise, yellow and black – in a repeating diamond design. An optical nightmare, but the bon ton of mid- to late Sixties. The skirt has an elasticated waist (about the first time you see this on clothes). Label: 'This garment is made from 100% Turbo Orlon* *Du Pont Regd. Trademark. It is recommended that this garment be hand washed. Made in England'. Not quite so easy care as we thought. Unusual. About 1964. £25-30/$40-50. (See Plate 10.)

Coolie-shaped beach hat decorated with rows of bright orange, fluffy nylon fringe. Label: 'Baby. Made in Italy'. About 1966. £12/$20. Wicker basket shaped like a gondola – there were thousands of these about. 1960-65. £10-15/$17-25.

Wonderful one-piece bathing suit with moulded bra-cups beneath a flesh-coloured stretch material overlaid with lattice of wide, black fish-net in a stretch chenille yarn. Label: 'Silhouette [a corsetry firm from the 1930s]. Bri-Nylon Bizarre Size 38'. This was still daring stuff in 1960 – at a quick glance, you would have thought she was starkers underneath. **£30/$50.**

VIVID BLUE COTTON BIKINI, trimmed with white broderie anglaise. The bra has under-wired and reinforced bust cups. Label: 'Silhouette'. About 1966. **£20.** Sea anemone bathing or posing cap/hat (you couldn't actually put your head under the water). Frills of nylon lace on a yellow base. Very Elizabeth Taylor. 1964-68. **£7/$12.**

BE PREPARED

I had written on my note-pad 'white pleated skirt' the moment before I popped out for tomatoes, and as I went by a local charity shop I spied (collector's develop amazing eyesight) on a rail a white, permanently pleated tennis skirt with zip side and 'grip-tape' waistband. Label: 'Perfit Sports Garment. Made from 100% Terylene'. About 1960. It cost me **£1/$1.65.**

A PAIR OF WHITE CORFAM shoes with chunky 2-inch heels, square toes and a very slight platform, with matching frame handbag. Label: 'Mansfield'. About 1968. **50p/80 cents each.**

PALE PINK ALL-OVER 'petal' cloche. My mother-in-law wore one like this at our wedding. A mistake. It was a think pink start to the decade. Label: 'Bermona Model'. 1961. **£25/$40.** (See Plate 10.) Bright pink layered feather toque with tuft of pink feathers on top. 1965-68. **£20/$33.**

W HEN YOU WENT TO A wedding, the mother of the bride usually wore something like this knee-length, lime green linen coat, lined with contrasting 'Italian-style' (Pucci influenced) abstact printed silk in pink, mauve and lime. Worn with a matching shift dress. Label: 'Susan Small'. 1966-68. **£30/$50 upwards.** (*See Plate 10.*)

HEAVENS ABOVE

Before she put on her dress, the bride's mother would have struggled into her Playtex girdle. This came rolled in a golden cylindrical box with a picture of a platinum blonde matron in a mink stole wearing one. To go with it would be the Playtex 'Cross Your Heart' brassière. Both these garments were supported by a huge

television advertising campaign in the late 1960s. As a matter of fact, a lace-making friend from Driffield sent me her old Playtex bra. It had had a run-in with a blue thing in her washing-machine, but it's still bouncy. Do you know the jingle 'You won't get to Heaven in a Playtex Bra / Cos a Playtex Bra won't stretch that far'? Well, this one might.

G LISTENING SUGAR PINK 'fancy' straw pill-box with top knot (very Jackie Kennedy – she seems to be wearing one in all those socialite photos). 1964. **£8/$13.**

L ARGE, UP-TURNED BRIM petal hat in various shades of light green with a 'swirled' crown, giving the appearance of a Webb's lettuce. Label: 'Rackhams of Canterbury'. About 1964. **£25/$40.**

T URBAN HAT MADE OF silk the colour of vanilla ice-cream. Label: 'Christian Dior Boutique'. In a Harrods box. About 1960. **£40/$66.**

L ARGE GREEN SILK CLOCHE decorated with a profusion of mixed flowers (very herbaceous indeed). Label: 'Edward French Edinburgh'. **£60/$100.**

E MERALD GREEN VELVET 'flower pot' hat decorated with a rhinestone brooch. No label. With two matching scarves. Charming. About 1960. **£12/$20.**

HAIR RECIPES

A really high, early 1960s beehive hair-do was created as below, according to the singer and entertainer, Mari Wilson.
Ingredients: Daily supply of extra-hold hairspray; electric rollers; plenty of back-combing; at least 50 hairpins; a flower in the pleat at the back.
Directions: Put rollers in. Take rollers out and backcomb until your eyes turn to water. Spray all over with hairspray, mould and grip – and pop in the flower.
    The other 'on your head be it' was a velvet hairband. These are associated with upper-class girls who were growing out the fringes they'd worn at school and who also wore Gucci shoes and Hermès head-scarves. The clip-on hairband could be tarted up with a flower or bit of net, and double as a teensy hat or bridesmaid's head-dress. After these gals relinquished the hairband (not all – they are still sighted in Wiltshire and Gloucestershire) they took to perching their sun-specs in the same spot.

P LAIN, ICE-WHITE, 'A'-line shift wedding dress, worn to just above the knee, in a stiff silk, fully lined, with sleeves that widen to a trumpet shape. The round neck and cuffs are banded with rows of rhinestone beads, pearls and gold thread. There is a long zip at the back and a pale blue bow has been sewn inside the hem (even modern girls are superstitious). Label: 'Harrods'. About 1964. **£40/$66 upwards.**

C HANEL DESIGNED THE original quilted leather satchel on a chain handle in 1930. It was known as a 'race bag': you had your hands free to drink champagne and mark your race card. Reputedly, the chain was there to foil 'cut-purses'. The quilted bag is an easily recognized classic that has been copied many times. Navy calf, quilted shoulder bag with side sections and snap-frame central portion. Lined with blue and cream striped silk with heavy, quality chain link strap and snap modelled as a jockey's cap. Label: 'St James. Made in Italy'. About 1960. **£50-60/$82-100.**

HERMÈS

Hermès dates from 1837, a shop in Paris that sold saddles and all the other leather accoutrements a well turned-out rider needed. It is now known for two main items, the scarf and the 'Kelly' bag, based on a saddle bag, launched in 1935 but renamed in 1955 after Grace Kelly, who often carried one.

    Scarves are much sought after and expensive. There are all sorts of wonderful scarves, lots with famous designer labels. The scarf, sometimes used as a stole, was often patterned in a revived Art Deco form, with strong colours and abstract designs. Jacqmar still did stunners.

A LARGE SILK 'SQUARE' SCARF with hand-rolled edge, printed in colours from deep blue to pale lemon and showing all things horsey – riders included. Label: 'Hermès'. About 1965. **£10/$17 upwards.** (*See illustration p. 135.*)

FLAT SILVER METAL MESH evening purse with Van Dycked edge (6 × 4 inches) and draw-up top on chain with finger loops. The short skirts brought a return of small, 1920s-looking purses. No label. Possibly Whiting Davies. Beautifully made. About 1968. **£4/$7.**

A SQUARE WHITE BAG with two handles made from long, faceted plastic beads with zip along the top edge. Inside were a pair of white Tricel crochet gloves and a pair of glittery sugar pink plastic earrings. About 1968. **£10/$17.**

TURQUOISE PLASTIC, 'bobble' bead satchel with self handle and snap-stud fastener tucked inside. (It had an unused make-up brush in it, too.) No label, but typical of the bags of the late 1960s. Slight damage. **£5/$8.**

CHAIN BELT MADE FROM gilt links and medallions of amber plastic. 1967-70. **£3-5/$5-8.** (*See Plate 10.*)

SHORT COAT-DRESS, SLIGHTLY 'A' line, in heavy twilled wool and Op Art design, with cream sleeves and collar, guardsmen red bodice with three large gilt buttons, and black skirt, two inches above the knee. No label. Looks like early Mary Quant. About 1964. **£40-50/$66-82.**

A LONG, SLIM-FITTING 'afternoon' dress in cotton voile with separate, frilled cape collar that ties, in shades of aubergine, mauve and sludge yellow. Closed by zip at the back. Label: 'Biba'. 1968-70. **£60-70/$100-115.** (*See Plate 11.*)

Many of his fabrics were designed by his wife, Celia Birtwell.

SHORT SHIFT OR SHIRT with long sleeves made from white cotton, printed with a geometric design in green, black and pink. Plain white cuffs and long pointed collar. Label: 'Ossie Clark'. He worked for Quorum, a Chelsea boutique, during the 1960s. He is known for his trend-setting styles, reminiscent of the 1930s. About 1965. **£45/$75.**

BIBA

Barbara Hulanicki, a fashion illustrator, married Stephen Fitz-Simon, an advertising executive; in 1963 they started 'Biba's Postal Boutique', opening a tiny shop, Biba, in Kensington to sell Hulanicki's exclusive designs. Biba attracted buyers from all over the world. The clothes were nostalgic – Art Nouveau meets Art Deco – inspired by early Hollywood. They were theatrical, vampish (lots of plum- and sludge-coloured crêpe and feathers) and, at first, very cheap. Biba produced a inimitable catalogue by 1969 when Hulanicki opened 'Big' Biba in the old Derry and Toms store in Kensington High Street. Biba is one of the most stylish labels from the 1960s and 1970s.

PAIR OF COTTON JERSEY camiknickers in a terracotta colour (and I have another pair in sludgey green), trimmed in lace the same shade. Label: Biba. These colours are typical of Hulanicki's palette. 1968-70. **£30/$50 each.**

RED LEATHER MINI-SKIRT with press-stud fastening down the front. Front fastening press-studs were a feature of many 1960s garments. No label. **£20/$33.**

PAIR OF SHORT, CANARY YELLOW, cotton/Rayon plush 'Hot Pants' with bib front (pocket centre) and cross-over straps. Label: 'John Craig'. John Craig was a well-known ready-to-wear label of the 1960s, specializing mostly in knitwear. 1968-70. **£20-30/$33-50.**

WORN WITH A NYLON SHIRT with large, rounded collar. White with brilliant pink and orange floral design. You'll find an array of disgusting, garish, synthetic blouses from this era. Likely they will have high street labels and long, floppy collars. They were around well into the 1970s. Label: 'Keynote' with washing instructions (these are seen by the late 1960s). **50p/80 cents.**

ABOVE THE KNEE, slight 'A'-line coat made from wide, horizontal bands of suede in rich shades of fawn to dark, bronzey brown. Eton collared, high fastened, back pleated and with discreet pockets inverted in a band. Label: 'Cherry. London'. About 1965. **£30-50/$50-82.**

The Arbiter of Good Taste totally approves of this little number.

ORANGE RAYON/COTTON, knitted-look, chenille mini-skirt lined with nylon with an elasticated waist. Label: 'John Craig'. £10. Worn with short-sleeved 'skinny rib' cotton sweater in horizontal orange and white stripes, the neck and sleeves edged in black. No label. £3-5/$5-8.

MINI SHIFT DRESS WITH white cotton yoke and cuffs and the rest in 'granny print' floral design of crimson, mauve, orange and green on a black ground. Zip at back. Label: 'Specially made for Dorothy Perkins'. There must have been thousands of copies of this dress. It is such a strong image of the late 1960s and early 1970s. But cheap quality minis are surprisingly rare, since they went out of fashion as quickly as they had come in, and you couldn't do much else with them. £25/$40. (*See Plate 10.*)

A POUCHED, BLACK SYNTHETIC leather peaked cap, a 'John Lennon' look-alike. John Lennon just took over the cap that was previously known as the 'Donovan', after the protest singer of the mid-Sixties. Before him, Marlon Brando had worn it, with a black leather jacket. 1968-70 £8/$13.

POWDER COMPACTS. Solid powder (foundation and powder mixed) was marketed by cosmetic companies from the 1950s in their own brand compacts. All the great firms did them – Elizabeth Arden, Revlon, Helena Rubenstein, Max Factor, Pond's and Miner's. They all used plastic: Goya had a lovely opaque shell and Yardley did 'Feather Finish' in circular plastic with their feathers logo impressed on the lid in 1958. You still find individual compacts for loose powder from the 1960s, but they are often deeper so that they could, if necessary, take solid powder as well, like the one I bought recently, which is nearly three inches wide with enamelled lid picturing 'Three Flying Ducks'. Label: 'Stratton'. About 1965.

THE MODEL BOX BAG was still carried in the 1960s, but now it was often made from fabric and was used as a handbag. Square box (12 × 8 × 6 inches) with zipper around the top, made from satinized cotton in bold floral pattern of bright green, orange and blue. Small handle on the top and lined in white plastic. Zipper broken. £2/$3.

T HE DESIGNER WHO TAUGHT us how a mini ought to look and who was the pivot of Swinging London is Mary Quant. Black, bonded acetate jersey, long-sleeved mini-dress with stand-up collar faced with cream jersey. Cream, centre front zip, neck to navel, and zips at the wrists. The skirt is cut in panels to swing out into a charming 'skating' skirt. Label: 'Mary Quant's Ginger Group'. About 1966. £100-150/ $165-248. (See Plate 10.)

MARY QUANT

Quant is a great designer. Born is 1934, her influence during the 1960s was huge. She was in tune with her own time and both the young and not so young loved her style. Although she did brightly-coloured clothes, too, her classic monochrome minis remain the bench-mark. Like Chanel before her, they were unaffectedly utilitarian. They were practical, easy, witty and elegant garments that could take you from Claridges (once they'd got over the shock) to the moon. Although expensive in their day, in my opinion, no one's done a better mini than our Mary. A Quant mini was typically worn with black, thigh-length boots with low heels, thick, ribbed or patterned tights (Quant), pull-down, slouch felt hats in either cream or black (cerise with black spots for weddings – see Plate 10), 'drives-an-E-Type' cut-out gloves and a small, chain-link shoulder bag. She also did stockings and tights (some of the earliest), underwear, PVC macs and make-up. Her famous logo is a stylized daisy. As the skirts went up to unmentionable heights, tights had to be worn to preserve a modicum of respectability. Among the many hosiery manufacturers who develped tights, some other names to watch out for are Wolsey, Brettles (did lovely lacey ones) and Aristoc. **20p/30 cents to a few pounds/dollars.**

A ROUND, BLACK, SYNTHETIC leather wig-box with loop handle and twist clasp, containing a polystyrene block with short-bobbed brunette wig marked 'Harrods'. Box marked: 'Fashion Tress Inc. Paris, Miami Beach, New York'. About 1968. £15-20/$25-33.

WIGS

As hats for young women disappeared, wigs became an alternative accessory. Hair styling now played a big creative part in fashion. 'Mum's perm' was definitely out for the young: they wanted to look like someone 'groovy' on the telly or like a pop star. The controlled, un-natural-looking hair of the early Sixties was replaced by sleekly cut bobs or long, sensual tresses. Hair was big news – even more so after the musical of that name. With a wig (and they could be hired) a transformed you could be presented by a quick trip to the Ladies.

FINE SILK SHIRT WITH LONG sleeves and pointed collar in an abstract pattern of deep pink, violet, blue and black. Label: 'Lanvin boutique. Paris'. A classy, psychedelic-inspired garment. Jeanne Lanvin was a designer born in 1867. She is famous for her charming 'mother and daughter' outfits, made early in the century. Her look was intensely fem-

inine. By 1927 she had introduced the chemise dress and a famous scent, 'Arpege'. There is a shade of blue, even now, that is called 'Lanvin'. Madame died in 1946 and the House was taken over by her daughter. 1968-70. **£30-40/$50-66.**

> I must now stop and go and eat a convenience supper that the vicar shoved in the Aga. We have to be social afterwards – an artist and his wife who live round the corner have asked us to take a glass of champagne with them. How civilized. The Arbiter of Good Taste has brightened up considerably, abandoned her studies and is getting ready to go to a party – wearing, apparently, deep mourning... with clogs.

A FULL-LENGTH EVENING DRESS, a high-waisted shift with 'v' neck and short sleeves edged with wide, gold sequinned braid. The material is alarming: gleaming silver and gold lamé brocade, in a 'crazy-paving' pattern. It looks as though you are wearing a moonlit path. Professionally made but no label. About 1970. **£12/$20.**

L AMINATED TEXTILE MINI COAT in a glittering, crinkle-effect gold and silver pattern, with wrap-over tunic collar, zip fastened on the left and lined with gold polyester. Label: 'Horrockses Fashion. By Appointment to H.M. The Queen, Dressmakers'. About 1968. **£40-50/$66-82.**

You were either in hard-edged black leather or metal at a disco, or dancing in mind-blowing patterned cottons or bright silks and velvets.

A SILVER LUREX (metallic woven thread material) mini shift worn with a sleeveless over-dress of wide silver mesh with a roll collar. Zipped at the back. This is typical of the metallic, space-age look; we visited the Moon in 1969 so we had to have something to show for it. I also have a 'Pacco Rabanne'-type waistcoat made of metal discs. No label. 1968-70. **£25-30/$40-50.** (See Plate 10.)

Mini-length, hooded rain-cape, in white and bright green PVC, with press-stud fastenings. Label: 'Mary Quant'. It rolls up into its own little carrying bag – which has the Quant daisy logo on it. It's very jaunty. About 1970. **£10/$17 upwards.**

Transparent plastic umbrella with yellow handle that opens into a big, curved arch to go over your head and shoulders. A most sensible design. **£15/$25.**

Pair of hipster trousers for a young teenager in navy brushed cotton, with a repeating snowflake pattern and Nordic-type red reindeers in snow at leg ends. Wide but not flared. Label: 'Miss Levi'. 1968-70 **£5/$8.** Vest top in fawn cotton jersey, printed with bunches of car keys on a tag. Label: 'St. Michael'. 1968-70. **20p/30 cents.**

Slim, high-waisted, long evening dress, the bodice with cap sleeves in cream watered silk, the skirt in turquoise silk banded with cream and trimmed with turquoise braid. Zip fastener at back. Label: 'Mary Quant's Ginger Group'; and another label: 'Miss Selfridge. Dry Clean Only'. 1969-70 **£30-40/$50-66 upwards.**

Miss Selfridge has always sold wacky, up to the moment, young clothes. I remember the excitement of first seeing this big boutique.

A pre-formed, latex-cupped, under-wired bra in red lace with detachable straps. Label torn (but she was size 36A). About 1960. **£15/$25.**

White, shaped, stiff nylon bra with under-wired cups. Very pretty, with a little pink bow in the centre. Label: 'Lovable'. About 1965. **£12-15/$20-25.**

A beautifully-made bra of black lace over cream net, with velvet cased under-wiring and a 'divorce' U-loop in the centre. Silk ribbon straps with elasticated 'spring' sections. She's a big girl. Size 40. Label: 'Cardolle. Made in France'. Madame Hermione Cardolle, who started the company, was a corsetière who designed a prototype bra in the early twentieth century, and the name still signifies exquisite underwear from Paris. About 1960. **£30/$50.**

A<small>N UNSTRUCTURED BRA</small> made from nylon and Lycra, floral patterned throughout. Label: 'St. Michael. Bust 36, Small Cup'. About 1966. **£20/$33**.

A 'HALF-BRA', UNDER-WIRED, in tinned-salmon pink lace with separate foam inserts that slip, discreetly, inside the cup linings for a bit more up-lift. Label: 'Gossard Wonderbra'. Gossard, an established corsetry firm, designed and promoted the Wonderbra during 1968/9 and it has done fantastically well – a good design, well marketed. It's difficult to say which are first editions, since they all look the same, but you must have a Wonderbra to boost your collection. About 1969. **20p/30 cents upwards**.

> Incidentally, as I was leaving a fund-raising luncheon recently, I was handed a note by a woman which turned out to be a little ditty that her husband had unearthed – sadly, unattributed:
>
> 'Oh, you can trust the foreign bust to thrust itself well forward,
> A charming trait that sad to say is lacking in West Norwood.
> In Palmer's Green la belle poitrine lies all too often fallow,
> Unlike the curves that one observes in Rome or in Rapallo.
> In Budapest the female breast is looked on as an asset,
> A point of view that's quite taboo in Bath or Wootton Bassett.'
>
> Since I got involved with undies, it's not the first, nor, I hope, the last rhyme I have received from a gentleman regarding the female form; but the vicar remains dubious as to their research value.

B<small>RIGHT PINK PANTIE-GIRDLE</small>, with a difference. A curious combination with a top part of power elastic, with a sheer nylon, elasticated-legged pantie attached and, as if that weren't enough, a set of suspenders attached inside. Label: 'Sihouette. Forever You'. About 1960. **£2/$3 upwards**.

P<small>AIR OF BLACK TRICEL</small> briefs, embroidered with the Lion Rampant holding the Union Jack and the words 'I'm Backing Britain'. Rare. About 1965. **£2/$3 upwards**. (What you want to look out for is a pair of Banlon briefs with a picture of the Beatles or the Rolling Stones on them.)

P<small>ANTIE-CORSELETTE</small> made entirely from nylon and Lycra, floral patterned in blue, green and mauve. Not a suspender in sight. Label: 'St Michael'. 1968-70. **50p-£1/80 cents-$1.65**.

POLYESTER MINI-SLIP with built in bra printed black with bright floral pattern. Hooks and eyes at back. Label: 'Etams'. Bra-slips were fleetingly fashionable – petticoats had a thin time during the Sixties. Rare. About 1969. **£3-5/$5-8.**

MARKS AND SPENCER made a similar thing, but as a dress. Mini-length, lined, high-waisted sleeveless shift, with wide boat neck, in bright orange and cream spot poly-cotton. It's intriguing for a collector because there is an in-built, soft-structured bra that does up first, under the zip. This is much as they used to make 'bra-dresses' in Jane Austen's day. Label: 'St Michael'. 1968-70. **£10/$17.**

BALL-GOWN IN A LOVELY shade of Cadbury's milk chocolate mauve, low necked, high waisted, with bodice and straps covered in *paillettes* (sequins) of glittering mauvey blue in a pansy design. The skirt is mauve viscose with taffeta underskirt. No label (cut), but could be a Frank Usher or similar 'good quality' evening wear. **£20-30/$33-50.**

WHITE, FULL-LENGTH sheath evening dress, with high neck, in white cotton piqué with 'lattice' decoration round the cutaway armholes. Label: 'Jean Allen. London'. 1966-65. **£15-20/$25-33.**

FULL-LENGTH, BLACK, watered silk dinner gown with fitted bodice and leg-of-mutton sleeves. The skirt is fullish and has deep pockets. Front decorated with self-covered buttons. Fully lined with zip at back. Label: 'Wallis'. Wallis had very chic clothes, including a range of 'Chanel'-inspired suits and coats. 1969. **£25/$40.**

SIMPLE, STRAIGHTISH KAFTAN with attached hood, made of heavy brown cotton with Indian embroidery. This is the time when the shaggy (smelly) Afghan coats came to our streets; if you want one of these you'll need a garden shed to store it in. 1968-72. **£10/$17.**

SMOOTH, FLUID 'COLLAR' necklace made from a panel of gilt metal links in a 'v' shape, which hangs in front like a bib and press-studs together at the back. No label, but possibly Whiting Davies Limited. 1968-70. **£60/$100.**

NECKLACE MADE FROM strands of silvery metal beads with large, star-shaped central pendant encrusted with brilliants and flanked by two large turquoise stones. Look like insignia. About 1968. **£20/$33**.

PAIR OF LONG, DANGLY earrings with champagne pink plastic orbs and pewter beads. There are sponges on the clips – they are very heavy and must have pulled her ears to shoulder length. **£8.50/$14**.

EARINGS

I don't have much 1960s jewellery, but earrings are the things to look for – getting larger and larger, either planetary clusters or beginnng to dangle. Ken Lane is the name of the 1960s and 1970s. Lots of big gilt medallions and pearls. Pearls were always in fashion and so were long beads, popular in an array of colours. Brooches were pretty big, and there were lots of animals – I've got a big green plastic parrot on my shoulder as I write. The style is generally bolder and more space-age than it was in the 1950s.

LARGE BLACK VELVET 'sailor' hat (15 inches across) with petersham bow. Label: 'Ektor Paris'. About 1965. **£20/ $33**. Red PVC, broad-brimmed hat with black rose. Label: 'Saks, Fifth Avenue. NY'. My granny would have said: 'Red hat, no drawers'. About 1965. **£15-20/$25-33**.

DARK PINK FELT 'HELMET' with visor front, decorated with two bands of cream petersham ribbon. About 1968. **£12/$20**.

RED, SHINY LEATHER, wide-strapped 'Mickey Mouse' watch. Label: 'Timex'. The motif is always in fashion – a timeless watch! About 1968. **£20/$33 upwards**.

DEEP CREAM CRÊPE trouser suit, with bishop sleeves, wrap-over top with flounced peplum and sash ties. The trousers are cut tight at the hips and billow into wide flares. Label: 'Ossie Clark'. 1968-70. **£70/$115 upwards**.

Long gilt chain with large petalled medallion. About 1968. £2. Gilt metal chain-link belt with pretend coins dangling from it. 1966-70. £12/$20.

Dark brown leather platform shoes with round toes, chunky heels and cut-out sides. Label: 'Chelsea Cobbler.' This was a trendy shoe label in the 1960s. 1968-70. £40/$66.

Chunky-heeled, sling-back shoes of yellow leather, the uppers decorated with large spots of orange and green. Label: 'Selby. 5th Avenue. Made in Spain.' About 1968. £10/$17. (See plate 10.)

Small, white corfam bag on chain shoulder strap, with gilt twist fastener. About 1968. £3/$5. (See plate 10.)

> The doorbell went at this point and there I found the wife of the man who runs the bicycle shop in Tetbury (a pedal above other bicycle shops since it holds the Royal Warrant). Sally, handing me a plastic bag, said 'I've been having a turn out. Would you like this? I bought it in London in the 1960s.' My dears, it is treasure! A high-necked, sleeveless mini-cum-tunic made of knitted string. Sally also told me she once wore a mini dress made from heavy silver foil — with purple tights — which looked wonderful, except that she clanked like the Tin Man.

Men's underwear 1960

Our man, bless him, has had to colour up to be noticed. A pair of fire-engine red Y-fronts. They're well used — a bit baggy. Label: 'Lyle & Scott. Jockey'. 1968-70. Unrealistic to put a price on them because, really, they're just ready for the duster box!

THE 1970S NOSTALGIA, DENIM AND STREET STYLE

I have never worn trousers, neither as a girl, nor since. I have never joined the bifurcated ranks of womanhood – except on one occasion, in the mid-1970s, after our house caught fire and my salvaged clothes either reeked of smoke or were sodden. For practical reasons, our plight warranted me donning a pair of denim trousers loaned by a friend. At the time, the vicar remarked that I looked 'unnatural', thus quelling any desire I might have had to add this garment to my wardrobe. However, trousers, and in particular denim trousers, can hardly be ignored by me because of personal prejudice, for they are the very seat of the 1970s.

Besides trousers, the 1970s caught hold of hundreds of different fashion influences, some of which permeated throughout society. 'Street Fashion' did not mean high street styles. It was from young people on the street of many different nationalities – some students, some not; some deprived, some not – that novel fashion ideas flowed upwards.

Seriously anti-fashion designers Vivienne Westwood and Malcolm McLaren set up their first anarchic clothes shop, Let It Rock, in 1971 at the wrong end of the King's Road, London. They sold retro Teddy Boy and Rocker clothes. Practically every year after that they changed the name of the shop, and the culture of the designs, but the basic shock-horror ingredients of sex and sedition kept customers buying. Although this deviant dress was at first bought by a minority (they never attempted to be 'in fashion'), it was pungently innovative. Westwood went on to herald many sub-cultured, street-wise fashion movements that have gained a place on the international catwalks.

Meanwhile, the styles of the hippies who had communed in their thousands at rock festivals took hold. Thus, kaftans, waistcoats, cheesecloth layers, flowers, beads and, of course, denim, went about their daily round, tripping up office stairs alongside more traditional, sober suits. But, in a short time, the hippy escapism, much diluted, became part of the retail fashion industry in the 1970s. Designer names that spring constantly to mind for 1970s fashion, besides the enduring Quant and Biba, are Zandra Rhodes, Thea Porter, Ossie Clark, Alice Pollock, Jean Muir and, of course, lovely Laura Ashley. As I write, many young people are finding retro Seventies-style clothes fun to wear *again* – the sort of things that when I see photographs of myself wearing them the first time around, I squeal, 'I can't believe I actually WORE that!' But we did.

CLOTHES OF THE 1970S

I'm certain that you are going to find tons of wonderful things from the 1970s. There are specialist shops, but start by going to a few jumbles, car boot sales or charity shops. Do remember to make friends with the ladies and gentlemen who run these shops: if you enthuse them, I'm certain they'll put things aside for you. Don't be sniffy when they do find something, but always thank them and buy it, even if it's not exactly what you want. They'll lose interest if you quibble; my house is full of 'Thank yous' in a good cause.

BROWN, FAWN AND RUSSET woolly, tam-o'-shanter hat with bobble on the top and long muffler to match. Long mufflers, like that worn by television's Dr. Who, were very fashionable during the 1970s. **£5 / $8.**

When I hung this on the back of my study door, the unrelenting horridness of it made the vicar beg me to write about it quickly and take it upstairs again.

A FLOOR-LENGTH MAXI-COAT made of uncut moquette (like a settee), patterned in shades of limey green and sludge olive, fastening with glittery bronzey buttons. Label: 'Sheraton. Fashion's First'. Quite honestly, this is supremely unattractive. Maxis were only around for a season or two, and you can see why. (Biba, however, did some super velvet ones.) About 1970. **£30-40 / $50-66.** (See Plate 11.)

A TYPICAL TROUSER-SUIT dating from the early 1970s. Short-sleeved, hip-length tunic, the trousers (wide but not flared) made from heavy, brocaded upholstery material in shades of gold, umber, yellow and sludge green. The guru-tunic has a stand-up collar and fastens with six bronze buttons. Label: 'Koupy'. **£45-60 / $75-100.** (See Plate 11.)

VELCRO

By the 1970s, the zip fastener was well established, but a new product began to be widely used. Velcro, invented in Switzerland in the early 1960s, consists of overlapping strips of fabric faced with micro-sized plastic hooks on one side and plastic 'fluff' on the other, which cling firmly together. What a boon it is to pantomime dames and young children who can't tie their shoelaces!

CLOAKS

In the 1970s, we also liked cloaks, in velvet and wool. They were all very romantic and Byronesque, but a pain when you had to dive for your bus fare. Mind you, the vicar still makes great use of his, particularly at chilly gravesides. Clergy dress is amazingly practical and timelessly elegant. Heaven help if the the Church of England abandons this unique dress for jeans and T-shirts.

PAIR OF CHESTNUT BROWN platform shoes, 4 to 5 inches high, with strapped and buckled uppers. Label: 'Chelsea Girl'. Chelsea Girl was a well-liked high street label of the time. 1970-72. **£2/$3 upwards**. (*See Plate 11*.)

PLATFORMS

By the late 1960s and early 1970s, high platform boots and shoes were worn by pop stars and others who wanted attention. The device was not new: in fifteenth- and sixteenth-century Venice, actors specializing in tragic roles wore buskins (calf-high boots with very thick soles) that definitely up-staged the rest of the cast. Female courtesans wore 20-inch tall chopines (slip-on shoes with lifts), dubbed 'cow hooves'. 'Your ladyship is nearer to heaven than when I saw you last, by the altitude of the chopine' is a chat-up line by Shakespeare.

NYLON SHIRT BLOUSE, with large, rounded collar and sleeves full at the cuffs. White with brilliant pink and orange floral design. Label: 'Keynote'. About 1970. **50p**. Acid, lime green shirt, very slim cut, with pointy collar. Label: 'Nicki Ferrari'. This luminous colour is cult for the 1970s. **20p/30 cents upwards**. Egg-yolk yellow viscose crêpe shirt with bishop sleeves. Label: 'Maggie of London'. About 1970. **£3/$5**. (*See Plate 11*.)

HIP-LENGTH, VERY NARROW, cotton jersey top in maroon, cut to curve over the tummy. Long trumpet sleeves and *bateau* neckline. Label: 'Deja Vu. Carnaby Street'. About 1970. **£2-3/$3-5**.

APULL-ON WOOLLY Noddy hat, also with bobble, in thick rib, double-knit, cream and brown, with matching muffler. Not the sort of thing you wanted to be seen in beyond a certain age. About 1970. **£5/$8**.

LEVIS

There are lots of different makes of jeans from this era, but the most famous 'old blues' are Levis. Levi Strauss was born in Bavaria and went to San Francisco during the goldmining boom of the 1850s. The bar-room story goes that a ragged miner challenged Levi (a travelling salesman handy with the needle? – no one's certain) to make a pair of pants that would stand up to the rigours of gold-digging. Levi was a fly boy, and cut his first pair from tent canvas, but later used denim, a tough cotton twill that came from Nîmes (*serge de Nîmes*). This was dyed indigo blue, and Strauss took out a patent for his design in 1872. Jacob Davies, a tailor from Nevada, joined Strauss in 1873 and together thay patented a garment

that had copper rivets at the gold-carrying stress points. The rest is history.

Really *old* Levis are as rare as gold-dust. A pair of 501s from the bad ol' days, complete with button-flies and rivets, would set you back a few dollars.

Denim is a democratic, totally classless material *until* you get to the label. The Arbiter of Good Taste has an immediate physical reaction to a jean label – usually bad. Considering its humble beginnings, denim now hangs out with a lot of dreadful snobs.

A PAIR OF WIDE-FLARED, mid-blue denim, hipster jeans. Label: 'Made in Heaven'. They have 'Heaven' tagged on the back pocket and have been turned up about 4 inches! 1970-74. **50p/80 cents upwards.** (*See Plate 11.*)

W HITE, LARGE BRIMMED HAT of transparent nylon 'straw', trimmed with white daisies. You find these hats everywhere – they were used for 'beach' and 'best'. About 1975. **£6-10/$10-17.** (*See Plate 11.*)

LAURA ASHLEY

Born in Wales in 1925, Laura Ashley at one time worked for the National Federation of Women's Institutes. She married Peter in 1949, and four years later formed a company to produce printed headscarves, napkins and tea-towels. In the late 1960s, Ashley designed 'rural' smocks (great for pregnant tummies) and 'pastoral' dresses, all in 100% cotton. Her famous, romantic looks are milkmaid-style dresses in floral eighteenth- and nineteenth-century prints

(thousands of bridesmaids wore them) and her 'Edwardian', white, tucked blouses. A brilliant, visionary designer, her work was a gust of fresh Welsh air to city high streets. Laura Ashley died after an accidental fall in 1985.

Lots of lovely Lauras around, but look out for early, simply styled examples. Women loved her clothes. Sadly, I believe the Laura Ashley shops of today have lost that comforting touch of Women's Institute 'Jam and Jerusalem'.

Hᴵɢʜ-ɴᴇᴄᴋᴇᴅ, ꜰʟᴏʀᴀʟ 'sprigged' indigo, white cotton dress, the bodice front completely diagonally tucked, the skirt not too full, with long sleeves, lace-edged cuffs, separate sash and zip at back. Label: 'ʟᴀᴜʀᴀ ᴀꜱʜʟᴇʏ. Made in Wales'. 1969-70. **£50-70/$82-115.** (*See Plate 11.*)

Pᴇᴀꜱᴀɴᴛ ꜱᴋɪʀᴛ, ᴠᴇʀʏ ꜰᴜʟʟ with double tier of frills in red/white stencilled cotton, with draw-string waist. The sort of skirt you went shopping in. Incredible, when I think about it, but rather splendid. Label: 'Laura Ashley. Dyers and Printers'. 1972-4. **£25-35/$40-58.**

Eʟᴇɢᴀɴᴛ, ᴛᴏ ᴛʜᴇ ɢʀᴏᴜɴᴅ, smock-frock in multi-coloured patchwork voile (lovely pinks, mauves and cerises) with cream smocked bodice and full, bishop sleeves. The skirt, which is layered, has triple frills at the hem (which makes in very heavy) and fastens, from the bosom, with 21 covered buttons and loops. Russian Gypsy look. Label: 'Tradis'. About 1970. **£25-30/$40-50.**

This was the Flower Persons basic kit — there was yards and yards of (cheap Indian imported) cheesecloth trailing around the British Isles.

Pʟᴀɪɴ ᴡʜɪᴛᴇ, ᴄʜᴇᴇꜱᴇᴄʟᴏᴛʜ, full-length smock, with the ubiquitous long sleeves trimmed with insertions of coarse lace. 1970-74. **£10-15/$17-20.**

Sɪʟᴠᴇʀ ʟᴜʀᴇx ᴛʜʀᴇᴀᴅ crocheted evening satchel with self strap and lots of fringing. Fringes were typical, applied to clothes as well as bags. About 1972. **£2/$3.**

Mɪɴɪ-ꜱᴋɪʀᴛꜱ ᴡᴇʀᴇ ꜱᴛɪʟʟ fashionable. A beautifully designed and made, very short, cream-coloured sleeveless dress and matching unlined coat in heavy textile lace with a daisy pattern. The coat, which fastens with a tie through two big metal eyelets at the neck, has a long, pointed collar, facings and dress bodice in cream viscose crêpe. Label: 'Richard Shops'. 1970-72. **£35/$58 upwards.**

Jᴇᴀɴ Mᴜɪʀ

Jean Muir (1928-95) was renowned for minimalist, flowing, nun-like designs in austere, dark-coloured jersey, suede or wool crêpe. But, occasionally, she did have strong patches of 'Scottish' colour. Muir always wore navy blue, which says a lot about her disciplined and simple approach to all clothes.

LIGHT, GAUZEY WOOL dress in glowing floral 'carpet' pattern of heather purple, blue, green, crimson and white, with long sleeves. An unfitted, just above the knee, shirt-

waister cum tunic with pointed collar and tiny self buttons. Label: 'Jean Muir'. Timeless. Not in good condition, but lovely to have an example of J.M.'s work, however damaged. 1970-80. £20/$33 upwards.

ALICE BLUE SATIN CRÊPE, 'midi'-length evening dress in 1930s style, with self covered buttons and loops on a guaged bodice. Designed with capped sleeves and skirt cut on the bias, giving an attractive up and down hemline. It is a most attractive dress. Label: 'Alice Pollock'. Second Label: 'Quorum recommend Jeeves Dry Cleaning and Valeting – 10, Pont Street, London'. Alice Pollock founded 'Quorum' – a boutique cum wholesale enterprise – and worked there with Ossie Clark. 1970-72. £40-45/$66-75.

A FULL-LENGTH, wrap-around-and-tie evening dress with short sleeves, 1930s style. Made in white moss crêpe printed with a sporadic floral design in red and black, called

'Round and Round'. Label: 'Ossie Clark for Radley' (cheaper than Quorum). Second label: 'Printed by Celia Birtwell'. 1970-74. £60-80/$100-132.

BRILLIANT RED, LONG-HAIRED fur fabric jacket. Label: 'Mr Darren. London W1'. Indescribable, really. About 1970. £20/$33. (See Plate 11.)

PAIR OF 5-INCH HEELED platform shoes with platform heels and ankle straps in patchworked look-alike lizard skin. Label: 'Derber'. About 1970. £40/$66. (See Plate 11.)

PAIR OF BLUE DENIM, 3-inch white plastic platformed mules with silver stars and stripes. No label. (Possibly American.) 1974. £25-30/$40-50. (Illustrated opposite, top.)

PAIR OF BLACK SATIN, ankle-strap platform evening shoes with square toe, decorated with a large, furled, black satin rose with two leaves. Label: 'K. Geiger'. These were mine, bought after my last son was born – a treat to have fantastic, dressy shoes after slopping around in flat ones. Actually, they were uncomfortable – the buckles ate into my ankles – but looked lovely if you didn't move. 1972. **£30/$50**.

PAIR OF SUGAR PINK, silk crêpe, fully-lined hipster 'loons' trousers, 34 inches around the leg-ends. Label: 'Annacat, 270 Brompton Road'. 1970-74. **£30/$50 upwards**.

WIDE CAPE-SLEEVED yellow cotton blouse with an A.S. Lowry-type print, with long pointed collar and sash tied at midriff. Label: 'Action at Marjaday. London'. 1970-75. **30p/50 cents upwards**.

YELLOW COTTON JERSEY 'angel' top – which is like a little smock, with high yoke, puff sleeves and a wide 'skirt' that came to about hip level. Zipper at back. Lots of these to be found very cheaply; I've another in pale blue cheescloth. 1970-72. **£2-3/$3-5**.

BABY BLUE AND WHITE checked polyester cotton, button-through 'angel' top or mini-dress, with halter neck ties. It is sweet, very feminine. Label: 'Dorothy Perkins. Warning Keep Away from Fire'. 1970. **£3-4/$5-7**.

CROCHET WAS EVERYWHERE to be seen, as in a hip-length, sleeveless tunic (or mini-dress) crocheted in gold Lurex yarn with laced front. 1970-75. **£10-15/$17-20**.

I know a woman who made her 1973 wedding dress and train from white acrylic wool in over 2000 rosettes on her 'Multi Needle' crocheting pins.

MIDI-DRESS IN biscuit-coloured polyester jersey with gathered skirt and bishop sleeves set into a low-necked, hand-crocheted bodice in fawn silk. Zipped at the back. Label: 'A Lewis Henry Original'. About 1978. **£10/$17**.

BRIGHT BLUE WOOL, long waistcoat made by hand from medallions of hand crochet sewn together. 1970-74. **£10/$17**. (*See Plate 11.*)

CUSTOMIZING CLOTHES

In the 1970s, it was considered the height of trend to have your blue denim patched, re-patched and patched on patched. Like old soldiers, such scars were worn with pride. Art students and other liberated souls began to write or draw on their clothes; denim was a good vehicle for this, the canvas for proclaiming unspoken thoughts, like a sampler. Artists like Jean Cocteau had done it years before and now it was seized on as a new form of self-expression. The young customized (some might say ruined) their clothes by 'reorganizing' them – cutting, slashing, painting and pinning them. The next stage, by the end of the Seventies, was to wear 'inappropriate' clothes to shock older sensibilities, a fashion that was at its height with Punk.

STRIPES WERE POPULAR, as in a long-sleeved, high-waisted midi-dress, with inset belt, in dark blue and white horizontal striped wool jersey, worked in chevrons on the skirt. Label: 'Garilee'. 1970-75. **£10/$17.**

SHORT, SMOCK-TYPE jacket made from indigo denim with long pointed collar, two patch pockets and turn-back cuffs to the three-quarter sleeves. Ideal to dress up your jeans. Label: 'Miss Selfridge'. 1970-74. **£6/$10.**

IMPORTED INDIAN DRESSES and skirts were enormously successful thoughout the 1970s. I have six or so in the collection. Muslin, cotton or silk, who can fail to be entranced by the beauty of the Indian materials? Typical is this heavy cotton smock with wide sleeves, in a wonderful mixture of russet and yellow, with beaded tassels. Label: 'Phool'. 1975-80. **£10/$17 upwards.** (*See Plate 11.*)

HIGH-NECKED, LONG-SLEEVED informal evening dress with sash of fine, soft Indian silk patterned in pink and gold border print. Label: 'Designed by Raksha of Hindimp for Liberty of London'. About 1975. **£3/$5 upwards.**

A BLUE STRETCH NYLON T-shirt with '1952 – 1977 Silver Jubilee' written across it. **£2-3/$3-5.** I also have a charming, unused silk scarf illustrated with 'E.R.' and silver coach and horses, taken from a design by Oliver Messel also commemorating this Royal event. **£6-10/$10-17.** Clothes alluding to important social events are worth looking out for.

UNDERWIRED, SLIGHTLY padded half-bra in glittery crystal nylon in shades of pinks, yellows and mauves. Label: 'Janet Reger Creations'. 1970-73. £15/$25.

PAIR OF BLACK LACE (polyester) French knickers. Label: 'Janet Reger'. About 1974. £10/$17 upwards.

BRIGHT ORANGE SILK and lace French knickers and bra (the bra cups made from swirled frills of lace). I feel this bra would have not worked well under a twin set – far too lumpy. It was designed for other, less formal occasions. Label: 'Janet Reger'. About 1975. £20-25/ $33-40.

INTIMATE APPAREL

Underwear? Either Victorian broderie anglaise layers, with slotted ribbons, or a tendency to stretch tight and easy care. Early 1970s still had lots of flower power and colour, psychedelic swirls and whirls. Knickers sported pop star images and bras blossomed with floral patterns. Seductive, alluring undies were still considered a glamorous speciality confined to Paris, the more expensive parts of London, or available only by mail order. Miss Reger has always done a stirring catalogue. When I was writing a book about stockings and suspenders, I was sent several, much thumbed, by a gentleman who said he'd enjoyed them.

LONG, FLAT, FRINGED and patched leather sack bag on shoulder strap. It is the much loved hippy fringe again. 1970-75. £6/$10.

FLAT, PAISLEY-PRINTED woollen cloth pouch, edged with lampshade fringe, with shoulder strap. Almost any material was used to make bags. About 1970. 25p/40 cents.

INTERESTING, FAIRLY LARGE, triangular-shaped handbag made from green chenille with an appliqué of branched trees on the front. Flap over top and shoulder strap. Lined with silk. Label: 'Anne Dudley-Ward'. 1970-74. £35/$58.

ANOTHER SHOULDER BAG made from soft, unlined suede with an oak leaf leather appliqué and beads on the front 1970-72. £10/$17. (*See Plate 11.*)

CURVED, SOFT SATCHEL in sludge-coloured patched leather with zipped top and front pocket with a shoulder strap. 1978-80. £3/$5.

> The vicar is back from Evensong and feels he's earned a gin and tonic. The Arbiter of Good Taste is not happy: it has been a Bad Hair Day, coupled with deep anxiety over an English essay. I have suddenly thought of all the ironing I haven't done and realize that I promised to look out things for next week's church fête.
>
> By the next day, the Arbiter has been mollified with promise of a new hairbrush and more styling ungents, and, strangely, this seemed to make the essay a lot easier to cope with. The ironing has also been dealt with and the vicar has a supply of black shirts for the week and I found a boxful of very odd things for the fête — some of which were purchased at the same event last year.

BLUE DENIM TAILORED shirt with 'w'-stitched pockets and pearl stud fastenings. Label: 'Wrangler'. About 1976. £5-10/$8-17.

TWO PAIRS OF UNWORN, one size 'Pop Socks', knee length and made to look like stockings, to be worn with trousers or long skirts. Label: 'Dorothy Perkins'. 1970-80. 35p/50 cents.

PAIR OF HUNKY, GREEN leather sling-back platforms with 4-inch cork heels. At the least cork was lightweight. Label worn. About 1972. 20p/35 cents upwards.

THERE WAS LOTS of back-to-nature jewellery — seeds, wood, shells and pebbles. Also ethnic, particularly Indian, pieces. The idea was that the jewellery should hang long, like your hair. Smart jewellery was streamlined, sleek forms in precious and non-precious materials. Long necklace made from looped metal and seed husks that dangle and rattle. 1975. 25-50p/40-80 cents. Also a turquoise blue and red bead necklace with large, round, beaded pendant. Definitely out of Africa. About 1970. 10p/20 cents upwards.

PLASTIC PACK CONTAINING a pair of fine gilt-framed, circular sunglasses with interchangeable lenses in pink, yellow, green and blue. This shape was made famous by John Lennon. Label: 'Samco. Italy'. About 1970. £5/$8.

MIDI-LENGTH, PURPLE DENIM pinafore dress with dungaree clips. Dungarees were very popular, particularly with young mothers-to-be. Label: 'Dorothy Perkins'. 1976-78. £3.50/$6.

QUILTED JACKET with toggle fastening in shades of mauve and dark blue in a paisley design. Label: 'Small Cotton. Made in India'. 1975-80. £5/$8.

A SUN-SUIT CONSISTING OF a pair of shortie shorts with pockets and a tie-around bra top in a deep earth red printed cotton. Label: 'Mausam. Paris. London and New York. Made in India'. 1970-75. £1/$1.65 upwards.

SKIRT-FRONTED SWIMSUIT made from nylon/Lycra jersey with inset moulded bust cups. It is patterned in a brilliant mosaic of turquoise, sea blue, gold, terracotta, orange and white. Label: 'St Michael'. About 1970. £2/$3 upwards.

NEW FACES

Make-up became as daring as you liked. Dress designer Zandra Rhodes' compelling *visage* is a retrospective example of this flamboyant skill. Swinging London psychedelia (clowns and colour) drifted into hippy glamour (David Bowie) which hardened into proto-Punk (Dan Dare with Sex) and then split to become embryonic hard Punk (studs and snarls) versus posers (frills and furbelows). They later became New Romantics, dressing like eighteenth- and nineteenth-century pirates and highwaymen. These people really painted; the face was yet another canvas waiting for artistry. Hoydenish colour was created by all the cosmetic manufacturers.

Upstairs in a drawer, I have dozens of plastic make-up containers, all shapes and sizes, including some that are triple-layered, from Revlon Inc. – lipsticks, glitter, shadows, eye-liners, shapers, blushers and blemish concealers. You could go for the works or do a natural look with lots of gloss.

A BRIGHT ORANGE, wide-woven corduroy (we called it 'elephant' in the 1970s), Spanish-style brimmed hat. 1970-74. **£5/$8.** (*See Plate 11.*)

P AIR OF BLACK, moss crêpe, hipster flares, slit to knee and edged with crimson ribbon, again in Spanish style. Label: 'Ossie Clark'. About 1970. **£30-35/$50-58.**

P AIR OF SQUARE-TOED, 'champagne gold' Lurex evening shoes with high wedge heels and T-bar straps. Label: 'Russell and Bromley'. 1978-80. **£5/$8.**

P URPLE CRUSHED VELVET, button-through tunic or waist-coat. Velvet, now revived, was a fashionable fabric. About 1970. **£5/$8** upwards.

A FIT-ANYONE, CAPE-LIKE evening dress of silver grey Tricel jersey, the material fixed to a *bateau* neckline with slits for the arms within the folds. Decorated with a knot of grey artificial flowers at the front neck. Label: 'Frank Usher'. Frank Usher was a designer of beautiful ready-to-wear evening and dress-up clothes. The name has been trading since the late 1940s. The dress is a good copy of the Japanese *couturier* 'Yuki', known for his sculptured, one-size draped dresses of the mid-1970s. About 1978. **£12/$20.**

We loved craft knitting – by hand or by machine. Elegant machine-knitted clothes were popular by the mid- and late 1970s.

O ATMEAL WOOL AND LINEN mix knitted 2-piece. Midi-length skirt with lacy edge and a pearl-buttoned blouse cum cardigan with lacy collar and cuffs. Label: 'Mary Farrin'. Apart from the danger of looking looking like a bowl of porridge, it is a charming outfit. Mary Farrin was a leading light of 'dressy' knitwear. 1978-80. **£4/$7.**

W EDDING DRESS MADE from ecru pleated polyester chiffon, sprouting from the neck in a tiered design over a self-coloured foundation. Decorated with a collar of flowers, the gown has ties at the nape and each wrist. This dress, which the Arbiter thinks is too lampshade for words, has both Yuki and Gina Fratini *somewhere* in its sights. Label: 'Jean Varon'. Another firm specializing in ready-to-wear copies of *couture* clothes. Probably worn with a little cap, dangling ribbons and flowers, and no veil. 1978. **£25-30/$40-50.**

A SLEEVELESS, CALF-LENGTH polyester silk tent with a frilled neckline. Huge, vivid pyschedelic pattern in blue, green, orange, gold, mauve and white – with pockets. It would have been worn with very gold accessories – including strappy sandals – just right for the Greek Islands. Label: 'Frank Usher'. Perhaps not one of his best. 1970-72. **£5-10 / $8-17.**

Over-large patterns are a feature of dress materials in the mid- and late 1970s. Lots of big statements on small occasion clothes.

P AIR OF CHUNKY TAN leather 'loafer' shoes with slight platform and high, stacked leather heel. Label: 'Dolcis. Sports Girl'. About 1978. **£3.50 / $6.** (*See Plate 11.*)

SPORTY STYLES

Another influence on dress in the late 1970s was health and fitness. Now, I have not made a conscious effort to collect 'gym clothes', but be aware that they were becoming increasingly 'label' marketed (the USA started it, of course). The tracksuit was easy to put on and a must, whether you jogged or not; and aerobics, eurythmics and dance-based activities required Lycra leotards and footless, all-in-ones. It's interesting that the sexy, colourful stretch gear was there, ready and waiting for the amateur, as a hundred years' worth of professional dancers had worked out in black cotton jersey, with hand-knitted cross-overs and chunky leg-warmers. Those leg-warmers certainly grabbed high streeters trotters – in the late Seventies, they were donned by girls who didn't know a *pliié* from a knee-bend. They exercised, in their way, to the instructions on special records.

MEN'S UNDERWEAR 1970

A ND HIM – WHAT A TURN UP for the book. Unisex knickers: bikini-sized, blue, horizontally-striped red, white and black cotton jersey. This garment is what is known to gentlemen's outfitters as 'a slip'. This pair, much worn, full of small holes, was sent to me by a kind man who answered a personal ad. asking for gentlemen's old pants that had I placed, in all seriousness, in the *ChurchTimes*. Label: 'St. Michael'. About 1975.

THE 1980S POWERFULLY GEARED

At a Ladies' Circle luncheon a few weeks ago (a 40th anniversary, lovely balloons), some of the ladies were chatting about the Eighties. They recalled the wedding of the Prince and Princess of Wales in 1981. I mentioned the Greenham Common women of much the same time, but that didn't draw comment; nor did Madonnna's first bra — well, her first *talked* about bra — a sensational *diamanté* job designed by Jean-Paul Gaultier for *Girlie Show* in 1983. No, it didn't ring any bells, whereas Joan Collins' 'Alexis' character in the television series *Dynasty* was vividly remembered and exclaimed on. Glamorous, fifty-something Joan, in her smart little suits and high heels — they remembered her. Glitz, glamour, gold braid, big shoulders and designer labels are possibly the fast-dyed images from the Eighties.

'I'm doing nicely, thank you' factions wanted good clothes, possibly better than their parents had had, and they were prepared to pay for them. They travelled and bought clothes abroad. Designers and manufacturers of everything from clothes to luggage realized that the *nouveau riche* felt confident letting others know what and how they bought — so labels worn on the outside were not only acceptable, but conditional.

Traditional class divisions had broken down, but money, or lack of it, formed its own, rigid class structure. Poor, out of work youth could wear exactly the same as middle-class undergraduates, but they probably didn't. Impoverished inner cities created a sub-culture of street youth with nothing else to do but become self-absorbed. The frustration felt was proclaimed by their 'protest' clothes. (This is not a new idea – the Sans Culotte, Marcaronis and Incroyables had done much the same in late eighteenth-century France.) Punk (meaning rotten or rubbish) is one documented fashion and skinhead is another. Punk is flagrantly sexual, a hideous send-up of taboo areas of clothing such as black leather, bondage, studs, slashes, pins, piercing, tattoos and outrageous warrior hair; skinhead is arrogantly aggressive and menacing, with shaved heads, more tattoos, collarless shirts, braces and short or rolled-up trousers showing shin-kicking 'Bovver Boots'.

Of course, the ladies of the luncheon circle didn't mention any of this either, but, for a fashion historian, it's interesting to note the way that during the Eighties (and 1990s) this 'out-cast tribes' look was garnered by several wacky international *haute couture* designers. Ironically, the 'withouts' were unwittingly creating a fashion for the 'withins'. It is a dark background to the meritocratic, grasping, greedy, flashy 1980s.

CLOTHES OF THE 1980S

It's pouring with rain – the vicar feels concern about the fête tomorrow; it takes place in the beautiful garden of one of our parishioners (surely, most kind of her), but it is always a problem if it rains. All that knitted craft, all those White Elephants, not to mention the cake stall and the strawberry teas. One year someone had a brain-wave and set up an umbrella stall.

I'M GOING TO START WITH Diana, Princess of Wales and one of the flotilla of high street fashions she launched. Polyester cotton blouse in fine stripes colured red, blue, yellow and white, with pie-crust frill at neck and wrists. These were leftover from the Princess's carefree, Sloane Ranger days before she married – and women everywhere copied her. Label: 'Debenham's'. 1981-84. **25p / 40 cents upwards.**

ROYAL WEDDING 1981 polyester silk head-scarf in shades of pink, white and yellow, illustrating Highgrove, the Prince of Wales' country house in the Cotswold town of Tetbury. **£10-15 / $17-25.** The Princess set the bench-mark for The Biggest Wedding Dress You Can Cram Into A Coach look. I have a diaphanous, ice-white sprigged nylon one decorated with false white flowers. Very, very full skirt and underskirts set from a low waistline, with flounces at neck, sleeves and hem – which is edged with a flexible *rouleau* of satin-bound wire. It moves like a tidal wave. Label: 'Yumi Katsura, Paris, New York and Tokyo'. 1981. **£50 / $82.** (*See Plate* 12.)

HAIR, WHICH WENT to gleaming straight by the end of the Eighties, makes me think of 'Scrunchies', fabric-covered elastic bands which girls seemed to wear as bracelets as much as hairbands. The Arbiter has a basket full of 'Scrunchies' and wide 'Fergie' (Duchess of York) hair bows.

WEDDINGS

What can I say about these extravagant 1980s wedding dresses? They are very pretty in a Cinderella way, there's just such a *lot* of them. The spiritual grace is replaced by a conspicuous consumption. The vicar often says, 'the bigger the dress, the smaller the marriage'. The further society moves away from virtuous behaviour (let's not be coy, few virgins are led to the altar these days), the more spectacular the bridal array. 1980s brides often verged on pantomime.

The Princess of Wales' going away hat was truly delightful. Designed and made by Royal milliner John Boyd, it was a 'reflection' on a jaunty riding hat,

a style originally worn by Empress Eugenie and another Princess of Wales, Alexandra in 1863. It is a small, curl-brimmed, pink straw bowler with three long white ostrich plumes laid jauntily across the crown. *(See Plate 14.)*

This was a winning hat, in every sense. I had a replica made by another milliner, Joan Walton Spooner, for the collection, but Mr Boyd's hat launched millions of high street copies. Little straw pill boxes, bowlers and pork pies with a bunch of feathers perched on the back were seen bobbing about at every wedding reception and hatty do. You'll find them for a few pence or a few pounds.

DRESS OF CHARCOAL GREY, tie-dyed cotton, ripped and tattered, an 'Anti-Nuke' shift covered in Greenham Common Peace Campaign badges. Designed and made by a student. 1981-82. Prices are difficult because, as yet, no one knows. Probably £20-30/$33-50 for the dress and £60-80/$100-132 for a collection of rare badges (or £3-5/$5-8 each). Also a tie-dyed (mauve, the colour of suffrage) dungaree suit, a pair of leather sandals and a banner from the first Greenham March in 1981. £50/$82.

DOC MARTENS

Greenham Women, without realizing it, made a fashion contribution. Besides tie-dye and denim, cold weather saw hooded parkas, camouflage jackets, fingerless mittens, baggy trousers, 'Damart' undies, and, of course, 'Doc Martens' boots. I have a pair of these in the collection – the higher the lace-hole count the more aggressive the tone. This pair belonged to the Arbiter, but 8-ups are pussy-cats compared to some. 15-ups and you're trouble.

Dr. Klaus Maertens, an orthopaedic surgeon, damaged his foot when skiing, so with his university pal Herbert Funck,

an engineer, he developed the first air-cushioned footwear in 1947. But it took an English shoe manufacturer, William Griggs, to realize the true potential; he bought exclusive rights to the product, anglicized the name and the first boots marched off the assembly line in 1960.

ANKLE-LENGTH, WHITE COTTON sheath dress, with tying shoulder straps and tabard over-skirt. Decorated with cut-outs, embroidered blue. Label: 'French Connection'. Early French Connection clothes are well worth collecting. Simple and wearable. Made in India. About 1984. **£10/$17.**

BLACK COTTON JERSEY/polyester T-shirt dress with screen-printed woman's face and hair in green and silver. About 1982. **£3.50p/$6.**

KNEE-HIGH, SHINY BLACK leather boots with straight, 4-inch pointed and stacked heels. About 1980. **£8-10/$13-17.** (See Plate 12.)

PAIR OF WHITE CALF SHOES with kitten heels and bow trim on cut-out heel. Label: 'True Form. Dorian'. About 1984. **£3/$5.** (See Plate 12.)

PAIR OF VERY DARK GREEN/RED tapestry, mid-calf, lace-up boots with extremely pointy toes and spikey heels. Lovely material, leather lined and well made – on plastic soles. Dance club wear, probably owned by a Goth, of the early 1980s. **£28/$45.** (See Plate 7.)

GOTHS

Ghoulish and ghostly Goths were another style tribe, who emerged from their crypts and caves in the early 1980s. They had dead white pancaked faces with eyes and lips slashed black or blood red. Hair was jet black and combed up to a fright. They never smiled. The girls wore black velvet, cobwebby net, lace mittens and leather tinged with purple, green and red, very heavy silver jewellery and, always, steeple-pointed shoes and boots. I think it's my favourite anti-fashion, because it is so feminine.

BLACK, WIDE SQUARE MESH, collarless shirt with tails. It does up with black studs down the front. Two breast pockets, shoulder epaulettes, all edges and seams picked out in luminous turquoise nylon. 1980-85. **£10/$17.**

FAKE FUR COAT, WORN to the knee, belted or buttoned, with matching hat. It's a bit teddy bear looking, in browns and cream. Label: 'Bickler'. 2nd label: 'Important Do Not Dry Clean. Do not Steam or Heat this Garment.

Clean only by the Furrierized Method'. Real fur was drummed out by the 1980s. Animal lovers, the eco-aware and the young chose not to wear real fur. About 1980. **£12/$20**.

Classic latex rubber sheath, laced through metal eyelet holes at the back (or is the front?). There's not a lot you can say about it except that it is dreadfully difficult to store (it sweats) and has to be dusted over with talc every now and then. From a bondage shop. 1984. **£85/$140**.

Every late twentieth-century collection ought to have a bit of rubberwear, and its essential dog-collar and hand-cuff accessories. I joke not. Fetishism and fantasy were finding outlets; from furtive beginnings, rubber became part of an international, hermaphrodite dress culture.

Leather jerkin with a huge plastic zip up the back and set with two copper cones for the bosom. Such crudely sexual clothing identifies something of the Eighties. Bordello wear was moving from the underworld to up-market catwalks. Fashion, like a bored child, was getting naughty. About 1984. **£50-60/$82-100**.

A three-quarter length 'swing' coat, with two pockets, made from plastic-coated material. It has baseball player shoulders (door-post to door-post) and is spray-painted in silver, moon blue and stencilled in black stripes and, oddly enough, Tudor roses. It takes some beating for uglification. Label: 'Siren. Designed in England'. 1985-88. **£4/$7**.

Large, black, polyester/jersey T-shirt (free size) with padded shoulders and decorated on the front with gold beads, jewels, stars and stripes and written in gold lettering 'American Dream'. Label: 'Spring Dew'. About 1988. **£3/$5**.

Big, white, silver lurex machine-knitted jumper with mammoth shoulder pads. The front is decorated with huge white satin appliqué of a horse's head and sprays of silver net and lamé radiating from it. It is hard to imagine that this style will ever be revived. Label: 'Alexandria'. 1988-90. **£3.50p/$6**.

A BLACK AND WHITE, hip-length, casual jacket, with pockets, padded shoulders and cut with a curved front with ribbed edging. It is patterned sweat-shirt material in a 'jungle' print and two panthers are encrusted with black sequins with red paste eyes. Label: 'Pierre Cardin. Paris – London. Made in Hong Kong'. 1988-90. £7/$12.

T-shirts would make a wonderful collection on their own. Queen of T-shirts is designer Katherine Hamnett, who took the subversive street element and made it billboard bold.

B IG, BLACK, COTTON T-SHIRT, screen printed with a grisly picture of a girl, gun and blood on the front. On the back: 'Safe sex, designer drugs & and the death of rock 'n' roll'. Label: 'Screen Stars by Fruit of the Loom'. 1988-90. £5/$8.

W HITE T-SHIRT WITH picture of Minnie Mouse on the front. Such characters were worn by adults, too. Label: 'Disney Character Fashions'. 1980-84. £3/$5.

Mrs Thatcher as Prime Minister was a strong image. This created an era of Girls in Lapels. Seriously emancipated females wore mannish business suits.

D ARK GREY, CHALK-STRIPED, double-breasted, 2-piece suit. The square-cut jacket, allowing nothing for female curves, has three pockets, wide lapels and shoulders that could carry a takeover. The skirt is straight and short. With it she would have worn high, straight heels and carried a briefcase and a big, top-stitched leather handbag on a shoulder strap. In the evening she probably went out clubbing in a rubber dress. A good example of male clone dressing of the early 1980s. £4/$7. *(See Plate 12.)*

P AIR OF BLACK, RIBBED silk court shoes with pointy toes and straight, triangular-shaped 4-inch heels in emerald green satin. Label: 'Yves Saint Laurent. Paris.' 1986-90. £3/$5.

S ILK 2-PIECE, STRIPED in vibrant orange, purple and black and white spots. It's an unfitted, long-sleeved blouse top, draped at the neck, and knee-length pleated skirt with wide, matching, buckled belt. Now, although this is shuddermaking, it also demonstrates how *couturiers* went with the American television star look. Label: 'Givenchy Nouvelle Boutique. Paris'. About 1984. £20/$33. *(See Plate 12.)*

B ELTS WERE VERY ELABORATE and waist cinching at this time, to balance the width of the shoulders and fuller skirts. Bronze gold, 2-inch wide belt with large, elaborate gilt buckle. Label: 'Jane Shilton'. 1986-90. £2.50p/$4.

ONE-PIECE SWIMSUIT in black and fluorescent (safety) green top with plastic zip to front. High cut legs, low cut arms and 'sports' back. Front lined. Label: 'St. Michael'. Second label: 'nylon/polyamide/elastane Lycra/polyure-thane': it's got the lot. 1998-90. **£7/$12**.

I'LL DO A SHELL-SUIT NOW and get it over with. Slate grey, with lime and sand streaks (mountain colours) shell-suit in a crinkly nylon 'tent' material. It is lined with cotton jersey and looks totally weather-proof – and probably non-biodegradable. No label. 1988-90. **£3/$5**.

You have to be brave and keep one in your collection (not neces-sarily indoors — it would be happy in a garden shed).

SLIM, CLUTCH-SHAPE, 'cream' reptile skin and leather hand-bag. Very heavy frame with antiqued clasp and small, smooth chain handle. A really nasty accessory, which would have cost a fortune at the time. About 1980. **£6/$10**.

FLAT, PALE BLUE LEATHER envelope bag (14 × 8 inches) with stud fastening. The Princess of Wales, determined not to be lumbered with a handbag like her Royal mother-in-law's, proceeded to keep one of these tucked under her arm, even when having bouquets foisted on her or tackling the hugs of boisterous children and other admirers. Thus a fashion was created for these bags during the Eighties. Label: 'Made in Britain'. 1982-86. **50p/80 cents**.

A COUPLE OF SPANISH (I guess) eco-no-no handbags from the early Eighties. Both large: one a sac closed with a zip with a shoulder strap; the other a two-handled 'Kelly' bag. Both are in pony skin: black and white and brown and fawn. Ugh. **£1/$1.65 each**.

PINK, 'LATTICE', MOULDED plastic basket stamped 'Mon-Sac'. Made in Spain. The Arbiter used to carry all her Saturday ballet togs in this. The ultimate in synthetic material chic. 1987-90. **50p/80 cents**.

CERISE SUEDE FABRIC, small duffle bag, brightly embroidered with a big sequinned elephant in the middle. Very Indian. 1984. £1.50/$2.50.

DENIM SATCHEL BAG with moulded amber plastic handles and long, dog-lead, clip-on strap. About 1985. £1/$1.65. Large, tapestry, metal-framed Gladstone bag with leather handle and clip-on leather strap. 1988-90. £1.50/$2.50.

DULL GREY COTTON SMOCK with beige tape on seams and collar which ruches up on draw-strings. It is a drab, almost penitential garment. Label: 'In-Wear design – Kirsten Tiesner'. 1984-86. 30p/50 cents.

HEAVY, CHARCOAL GREY, hand-knitted swing coat with padded shoulders and decorated with hand embroidery in white and gold in a trailing floral motif, including all the borders. Label: (indecipherable, apart from 'Made in Yugoslavia' and the Wool Symbol). 1980-85. £20/$33.

BLACK, FINE WOOL, high-necked blouse with bat-wing sleeves, teamed with matching full skirt and long stole in a beautiful grey-blue, hand-woven tweed. Label: 'Jean Muir'. About 1980. £35/$58.

INCREASINGLY SOPHISTICATED women sought hand-crafted fashion goods, including beautiful scarves – painted, woven or screen printed. These seem to grow in size as the decade progressed, so by the late 1980s they were thrown around the shoulders over suits and coats. Black fringed shawl cum scarf or stole, woven with a floral design in puce, cerise, bronze and green. Label: 'Glentex. 100% Acrylic. Made in Japan'. About 1988. 25p/40 cents.

JEWELLERY

Extravagant dazzle was intrinsically part of the era, with designers like Butler and Wilson of London producing enormous costume jewellery sparklies by the mid-decade – lizards, spiders, slithery snakes, sunbursts, hands, faces, champagne glasses and vast collars. There were lots of coral, amber and other natural semi-precious stones, and many young jewellery designers were creating wonderful pieces from non-precious materials. Earrings were long, elaborate chandeliers to compete with big hair and shoulder pads.

RED, BRUSHED COTTON, bat-wing sleeved dress with dropped waist and short, gathered skirt, Peter Pan collar and self-belt. About 1988. **£2/$3**.

FULL-LENGTH, GLISTENING grey/white and silver-spangled net ball-gown, with big puff-ball sleeves and low-necked, black velvet 'Cinderella' bodice, zipped at the back. A dress that owes much to the fairy-tale look initiated by the Princess of Wales's early 1980s evening finery. Label: 'Gina Fratini'. About 1985. **£21/$35**.

ONE OF MY DAUGHTERS, who became a dancer, has left me the legacy of the following clothes for the collection. They are all from the 1980s. Nothing is yet valuable, but all are significant to the time and the owner. Baggy, sea green, woollen all-in-one leggings with braces. A Snoopy-motif, reversible sweat-shirt. A big, one-size T-shirt in black, terracotta and turquoise, stencilled 'French Connection'. A black and white striped rugby shirt that had belonged to a boyfriend. A short, full, terracotta cotton jersey 'Ra-Ra' skirt. A black cotton jersey, long-sleeved top with a small collar that has a 1914-18 girl's face screen printed on it and, on the back, the words: '*Imagine the early days of this century, a romantic, nostalgic breeze from a past time. An old photograph, telling it's own story... A young girl looking out in nowhere... with her mind in somewhere else... long time ago...*' Midi blouse and short, full skirt with wide waistband in grey cotton, border-printed in bold florals – dark blue, green, orange, yellow and mauve. Label: 'French Connection'. White T-shirt with screen-printed picture of 1930s children sitting on a wall eating buns. Label: 'Jeffrey Rogers'. Searingly bright, cerise pink and lime green cotton jersey long tunic and bicycle shorts. Label: 'Pamplemousse'. Two pairs of black leggings. One pair of slashed and cut-off denim Levi jeans patched with pink flowery material beneath. And a large basket.

THE NEW AGE TRAVELLER daughter dumped all these items when she finally took off. A dark grey jumper, the sleeves now so long you could use them as restraints. Each wrist has thumb-holes – teenagers work with about half an inch of fingers showing. A black PVC bum-bag. A big T-shirt with the word 'Nasty' on both sides. Two tie-dyed scarves and an Indian silk one. A crystal on a leather thong. A Green Peace linen carrier-bag. A scarred black leather jacket that belonged to someone else. A pair of size 8 tap shoes. And a khaki satchel which she had inscribed when at school in the mid-1980s: 'Kill Tories' 'Frank Stinks' 'We All Love Maggie' (this scratched through in red ink) 'Brian is Rough' 'Kill the Tories... The Addicts' 'Billy Idol' 'I am out of this world' 'Wham Wham Wham Wham Wham' and 'Rodney is a Horny Bastard'. This wasn't an easy patch in vicarage life, but children are interesting, aren't they?

I must stop, because I can hardly see the screen and the vicar has another meeting to go to, so I must quickly slap the Aga with a few sausages. Happily, we hear that the fête has made several hundred pounds profit for the church funds – which is to be wondered at on such an un-summery day. The tombola took the most money; it always does, because church people like a little flutter. The teas came next. Looking round the stalls, I was tempted by a 1980s Jane Shilton bag and 1960s hat, a packet of National Trust Centenary Year (1995) notepaper, a British Hedgehog Preservation Society mug... and a pot of three-fruit marmalade. The vicar forbade me to bring home any rubbish.

PAIR OF INDIGO VELOUR court shoes with small, triangular heels and wing and buckle trim at heel. Label: 'Primavera'. About 1988. *£2.50/$4*. (*See Plate* 12.)

A BARBIE-DOLL SUIT, a rocket red denim designer 2-piece. Blazer-style, hip-length jacket with square shoulders, pockets and short, straight skirt. Sounds fine so far, doesn't it? But then comes the gold thread top stitching on every seam (including the hem of the skirt), gold thread buttonholes and a generous helping of gold buttons, shaped either as hearts or in the initials 'T' or 'I'. Label: 'Zang Toi. Made in New York'. About 1989-90. (*See Plate* 12.)

ANOTHER DIANA-INFLUENCED high street look. A 2-piece of ribbed polyester silk, the fitted, unlined white jacket (more a blouse) with puff sleeves and black button and bow worn over slim, above-the-knee, black skirt. Label: 'Dorothy Perkins'. About 1988. *£5/$8*. (*See Plate* 12.)

POLYESTER-COVERED, shallow white skull cap with contrasting wide brim of bright blue that curls up at the back with large stiff self-bow. Inspired by the Princess of Wales and a very flattering style. Label: 'Pronuptia'. 1986-90. *£10/$17*.

NAVY SKULL CAP WITH stiff transparent nylon net pleated into a frill, surmounted with bow and flowers sewn to the top of the crown. Label: 'Kangol Design' (known for their classic berets). About 1988. *£6/$10 upwards*. (*See Plate* 12.)

FASHION FAME OF THE 1980s

Popular labels: Levi 501s, Lacoste, Benetton, Gap, Adidas, Reebok, Nike, Timberlands, Hennes, Kanga and Next. **Designers:** Azzedine Alaïa, Georgio Armani, Body Map, Comme des Garçons, the Emmanuels (they designed Princess Diana's wedding dress), Katherine Hamnett, Kenzo, Calvin Klein, Jean-Paul Gaultier, John Galliano, Christian Lacroix, Issey Miyake, Thierry Mugler, Karl Lagerfeld, Ralph Lauren, Bruce Oldfield, Yves Saint Laurent, Catherine Walker, Jasper Conran, Margaret Howell, Gianni Versace and, obviously, Vivienne Westwood.

Haute couture clothes are mind-blowingly expensive by the 1980s and there is a huge divide between high street prices and those for a bespoke designer garment, so it's thrilling to discover a designer piece at a jumble sale or something.

They were still ripping jeans in the late 1980s, but it was more sculpted – the Arbiter tells me the cuts were horizontal, not vertical.

I did not shed a tear during the Service, but the bride, the Vicar and the Arbiter of Good Taste sobbed so much that extra handkerchiefs had to be handed up to them.

TWO-PIECE FITTED WEDDING jacket and full mid-calf length skirt in striped dupion (silk) in pale shades of cream, lemon, sage and heather. The jacket, with short peplum, has leg-of-mutton sleeves, a high neck and buttons to the waist. Label: 'Droopy & Brown'. It was worn by our eldest daughter, who married during a Sunday Communion Service. 1989. **£40-60/$66-100.**

ANOTHER DIANA-INSPIRED fashion was high-heeled (but not too high – she was taller than her husband) shoes with little bows on the heel seam. I have a pair in baby pink, with matching pochette. Label: 'Barratt's Shoes'. 1988-90. **£6.50/$10 for both.**

CLEVER FINDS

I think, apart from him, I may have dried up on the 1980s. Look out for Lycra leisure wear that has 'designer' labels on it and amusing pairs of knickers, such as Union Jack ones (souvenirs from both Royal Weddings) and ones with suggestions, such as the tiny bikini briefs showing two nautical flags and the words 'You may enter harbour immediately' which I have in the collection.

MEN'S UNDERWEAR 1980

PAIR OF BOXER SHORTS with a cartoon of the *East Enders* television series on it. Dirty Den, Dot, Roly the dog, Pat, Pete *et al*, set in the Queen Vic pub. Label: 'Spitting Image ©. London Clothing Co'. Found in a charity shop. They have never been worn. You can believe that this was one pair that no man has the stomach for, as evidenced by this cartoon caricature of Dot copied from the boxer shorts. About 1989. **25p/ 40 cents.**

THE 1990S LYCRA, LABELS AND FASHION VICTIMS

This is probably the hardest part of the book to write. There is something unreal about identifying and analysing the recent past. However, there are a number of indisputable dishes which have been presented in the decade's fashion menu.

Sports and leisure wear is the first example. Now, I implore all you first time clobber collectors, this is the stuff you are going to *have* to start gathering. All that colourful, jump for joy Lycra and Elastane is out there, stacks of it, and, even as a comprehensive collector of women's clothes, this is one stream of fashion that I have never plunged into.

In the 1990s, influences on fashion were fast and diverse. The decade's increasing awareness of environmental issues sparked a prediliction for natural fibres such as cottons, linens, silk and pure wool. Conversely, it also produced the most sophisticated man-made fabrics: Tactels, Teflons and stretchy Lycras. In style, the clothes swung between grand dress-up and comfortable, practical understatement.

Madonna, an icon of pop, showed us lots of herself, in and out of her underwear, and the fashion catwalks agreed that parading your underwear on the outside was totally cool. Charity shops were ransacked for out-moded piggy pink corsets and whirlpool-stitched bras, and the 'Wonderbra' came in for lots more well-advertised publicity and male approval.

In the young club scene, there were Ravers with smiley-face T-shirts, Cuties in little girl frocks and adherents of Grunge, a miserable, untidy, unbuttoned look that came from the U.S. in the early 1990s. It did just manage to crawl up the high streets, but it soon gave up, exhausted.

Television presenters appeared in very bright colours. Long jackets over short skirts was often the medium for these ladies, inspired by a certain Princess of Wales, of course. We have had lots of baggy tunics worn with leggings. In my opinion, this is one of the most unfortunate fashions ever. Hacked-away jumpers and bodices to show off (young) midriffs; over-stuffed armchair trainers with caterpillar tracks and tongues that loll out as if constantly thirsty; baggy trousers with tightish ankles, tight trousers with instep stirrups; deconstructed clothes, seams on the outside: all these we have seen. Desert boots, moccasins, plimmies, jellies, towering heels and platforms have also been viewed as the latest thing. And a workforce of opaque black tights strode through the land for almost a decade.

CLOTHES OF THE 1990s

It is almost impossible to give collecting prices for contemporary clothes, which are at the moment in the limbo-land of the lately discarded. Designer label clothes will always command higher prices than high street styles. You have to develop a sixth sense about what sort of clothes will be considered historically interesting or amazing in the future. It might be a humble garment that was not fantastically expensive or rare when new, but which represents a look that will be appreciated in years to come.

BIG, PLAIN, WHITE linen shirt with long tails. The fashion journalists used words like classic, preppy, Armani, Ralph Lauren to enshrine this. The white shirt was the clean, clever and cultured look of the New Nineties. About 1990.

PAIR OF BLACK PATENT lace-up shoes, decorated with suede cut-outs, designed with deep platforms and 7-inch splayed heels. The platform shoe re-asserts itself every couple of decades in the twentieth century. Label: 'Manic'. £70/$115 new.

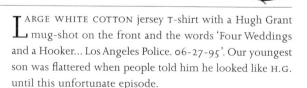

LARGE WHITE COTTON jersey T-shirt with a Hugh Grant mug-shot on the front and the words 'Four Weddings and a Hooker... Los Angeles Police. 06-27-95'. Our youngest son was flattered when people told him he looked like H.G. until this unfortunate episode.

SLIGHTLY FITTED T-SHIRT with cap sleeves and 'tails', bordered in a cobalt blue stencilled design illustrated with gold-painted, erect penis and 'Pagan V' on the front. Label: 'Vivienne Westwood'. 1990. £28/$45 new.

FAWN, SPECKLED BROWN, ribbed, ankle-length, sausage-skin dress with long sleeves and big roll collar. All acrylic. It might have been worn originally with a matching long, sleeveless waistcoat. This is the sort of sinuous, flexible look that designers like Bodymap first made successful in the late 1980s. 1994.

P LAIN FAWN, LINEN smock jacket fastened at the waist with steel 'fish' and 'horsehead' buttons. Natural-look linen, creases and all, has been revered throughout the 1990s. Label: 'Nicole Farhi'. About 1990. Worn over a plain black dress made of Tactel. 1996. £20/$33. (*See Plate 13.*)

C REAM/FAWN DUNGAREE pinafore dress with lots of pockets, loops to hang monkey wrench on, etc., metal slide-clips and metal stud buttons, stamped 'H' Casual Wear Division'. Label: 'Hennes'. 1995.

P ALE GREY/GREEN, viscose crêpe, tunic evening dress with a shirred 'elastane' bodice and long sleeves. Label: 'Ghost'. I love Ghost clothes. They will be very collectable in the future. 1994. (*See Plate 13.*)

S QUARE BLACK RUBBER handbag (14 × 12 inches) with hedgehog-like spikes over one side and a zip along the top edge. Label: 'Craig Morrison'. Craig does these weird and trendy things with rubber. About 1993.

The Arbiter had a fantastic duffle bag with spikes, but sadly its black degenerated to grey.

U NISEX, LEOPARD-PRINTED canvas ankle boots with black laces. They are luminous and 'glow' in the dark. Lots of animal prints ran around in the 1990s. Label: 'Converse All Star. Chuck Taylor. Made is the USA'.

P AIR OF BLACK SUEDE ankle-strap shoes with low heels. Label: 'Servas'. About 1995. £3/$5. Pair of gun-metal patent loafers. Label: 'Dolcis'. 1996. £4/$7. (*See Plate 13.*)

SHOES

Besides exclusively 1990s names like Cox, Westwood, Blahnik, Emma Hope, Jimmy Choo and Gucci (who did the talked about high, steel heel in 1997), are Yantorny (took years to make a pair of shoes in the 1920s and charged the earth); Pinet (established in the nineteenth century); Perugia (did spiral steel heels in the 1950s); Ferragamo (cork platforms and sling-back wedges in the 1940s); Vivier (beautiful evening shoes from the 1950s for Dior)

CHILD'S PAIR OF CLEAR, silver-sparkle plastic 'jelly' sandals with bows and green, pink and yellow 'sweeties'. Label: 'Ladybird'. 1996. **£4/$7 new.** (*See below.*)

PAIR OF INK BLUE PLASTIC ankle-strap sandals, the clear, 3-inch heel containing a tiny model of the Eiffel Tower in a silvery 'snowstorm' liquid. Label: 'Patrick Cox'. Patrick Cox is famous for his 'loafers' in the 1990s. 1996. **£24.50/$40 new.** (*See also Plate 7.*)

PAIR OF PATENT LEATHER, square, peep-toe mules, striped in mauve, lilac and black. Label: 'Red or Dead'. Bought by the Arbiter of Good Taste in 1996.

PAIR OF RAPACIOUS, nearly 5-inch stiletto-heeled, pointed court shoes in black and silver glitter. Label: 'Barratts Shoes'. About 1994. **£8/$13.**

PANDA BEAR WITH ROUND, red, zipped brushed nylon purse on his back, with webbing strap that buckles round a child's waist, extending from his front paws. About 1990.

A SMALL, HARD PLASTIC, floral-patterned egg-shaped evening purse on a black cord that hinges in half to reveal a black-lined interior. Label: 'Studio Accessories. Made in China'. About 1993.

A 'BIKER BAG' FOR YOUR Harley-Davidson chick. Hard, square, black rubber, stubbled like a cheesegrater, with sculpted chrome handle and rivetted metal front designed like goggles. Label: 'Hi-Tek Designs. London. Alexander'. 1994. **£65/$108 new.** (*See Plate 1.*)

BLACK, BARE-ONE-SHOULDER top, made from silk jersey decorated with sequins on the shoulder piece and a deep 'hip cuff' of scratchy black sequins. Label: 'Hilary Floyd. London'. About 1996. **£4/$7.**

Pair of bridal 'g'-string knickers with pink padded heart in front, tiny lace bustle at back. For added interest, if necessary, they play the wedding march when pressed. Label: 'Frederick's of Hollywood' (who have been doing naughty knickers since 1946, so they should know what pleases). Second Label: '100% acetate — exclusive of ornamentation. Dry Clean Only' (how inconvenient). 1994.

French knickers in shell pink silk, chiffon and lace trimmed, with matching chemise top. Label: 'Keturah Brown. London'. Keturah Brown has been a designer of deliciously feminine underwear for 25 years. Her work was selected to be shown in the 1997 'Cutting Edge' exhibition at the Victoria & Albert Museum, London.

Underwear

The strident look of Madonna subsided in the late 1990s and delicate, 1920s/30s retro underwear returned, mistily visible on the young under transparent summer wear. Big Knickers (to yer waist) were once more, literally, in *Vogue*.

Gun-metal grey polyester suit that looks like dull silk. Masculine image, with long, double-breasted, draped lapel jacket with choice of either a pair of tapered trousers or a short, straight, belted skirt. Label: 'Kello. Made in Denmark'. About 1994. £10/$17. (*See Plate 13*.)

Career Girl

The grey suit is what I like to call the Investigative Journalist's kit. Always ready wherever the action takes you. Strong feminist image. There's just a touch of the old-time tailor-made I suppose, but it's less tranquil. It looks very confident and unassailably tough (but, enigmatically, she may have got the shell pinks underneath). A good example of late twentieth-century career-girl dressing. Such suits are generally extremely well made, too.

White dupion silk 'hunting topper' with deep black velvet band and huge amount of veiling. Label: 'Herbert Johnson. London'. Herbert Johnson, an established gentlemen's hatters, moved into millinery and created this sensational hat. It proved popular for weddings, and many brides went to the altar dressed as if for the kill. I bought this copy (for £285/$470) from H. J. as I felt it was an important statement in ladies' festive hats. 1993. (*See Plate 13.*)

Hats

Toppers and large, high-crowned, broad-brimmed, 1910-style hats have been favoured throughout the Nineties. Also seen were many versions of the upturned 'Paddington Bear' hat. Gilly Forge makes enchanting old straw hats with faded flowers on them which look as though they have been hanging around in garden rooms for years. I adore the soft, worn look of her hats. Deirdre Hawken is a jewellery designer cum theatre milliner cum embroideress, and her hats are minor works of art. She might make a hat designed like a cauliflower, a fish or a lobster. They are witty, 'Elsa Schiaparelli' creations, often using hundreds of beads, sequins, metalwork and specially dyed materials.

I wore one of her hats to our eldest son's wedding: he and his bride worked for *The Times*, so she made me 'The Thunderer' hat, a 'cage' of wire bound with dark grey chenille, trimmed with a bow of laminated and wedding-dated newsprint scewered on with a unicorn hat pin. Great fun. (*See Plate 13.*)

These would be expensive hats to find anywhere, but I have seen Gilly Forge for sale for about £30-40/$50-66. (*See hats illustrated in Plate 14.*)

T IGHT-FITTING, SHORT, stretch sheath dress in horizontal stripes of hot, 'African Sunset' colours with a black bra-top made from whirlpool-stitched cord with halter tie. Label: 'Helen Storey. Made from Polyester and Elastane'. The designer Helen Storey was a dancer, so she understands the sensuous movement of clothes. Her clothes are cerebral, original and timeless. 1992.

The Princess and That Dress

Speaking of posh nearly-news, may I mention that Princess again? The fact is, after the Princess's dresses were auctioned, I noted a dress she had worn the night the Prince 'revealed all' on TV – a short, black, strapless number with a shoosh at the side that the Press eloquently dubbed the 'Up You' dress. It was sold for £44,511 ($73,443).

This was the only off-the-peg dress in the entire auction, originally bought for a measly £1000 ($1,650); the designer, Christina Stambolian of London. On reading this, I tore up to the Costume Room to inspect the label of a stunning, 1980s black and white cocktail dress I'd bought only a few weeks before in a charity shop for £7.50p/$12. Yes, it does have a Christina Stambolian label. Oh, the feeling of triumph!

Christina Stambolian

DESIGNER NAMES

Important designer names from the 1990s to look out for are John Galliano (Dior), Alexander MacQueen (Givenchy), Versace, Prada, Paloma Picasso (jewellery), Oscar de la Renta, Valentino, Ungaro, Mila Schon, lots of Japanese designers (buy *Vogue* every now and then and see for yourself) and Stella McCartney (daughter of Beatle Paul), who made her design debut for the house of Chloe in 1997. But, as an innovator, I still go for Miss Westwood!

SILK SCARF DESIGNED by Gianni Versace. I bought it in a charity shop for only £2.50 a few days before the designer was murdered on 15 July 1997. As a result of his tragic early death, his designs become instantly collectable.

BREATHTAKINGLY SNUG-FITTING, eighteenth-century looking corset bodice in black satin and Lycra, stiffened with plastic strip-boning, zipped at the back and stencilled with a scrolling design showing a crowned orb and oak tree in gold. Label: 'Vivienne Westwood'. 1992. **£285 / $470 new.**

ANKLE-LENGTH BLACK SLEEVELESS sheath with bodice in wide bands of royal blue and white. Label: 'Top Shop'. Second label (sewn in the side seam at the bottom of the skirt where you don't immediately think to look): '95% Tactel 5% Elastane. Keep Away From Fire'. Like 1960s Crimplene, you must have a bit of Tactel in your collection for the Nineties.

BEAUTIFUL NAVY AND WHITE spotted, pure silk 2-piece with loose smock top and wide, palazzo trousers. Label: 'Annalena'. 1996.

A HANDBAG MADE FROM an opaque plastic Orb (hinged in two halves), surrounded by paste jewels in a circle of blue marbled plastic – the whole surmounted by a gilt, be-jewelled crown. Thin shoulder strap of leather. Label: 'Vivienne Westwood'. 1993. **£165 / $272 new.** (*See also Plate 1.*)

LADY JANE SPEAKS

Here is a frank interview with Lady Jane, my sixteen year-old godaughter, who is extremely clever, beautiful and goes to a local, all female, high school:

'I wouldn't buy anything that doesn't have a label, but it has to be the right label or I'm not interested. Sometimes I've bought it even though I didn't really like the thing itself, but I know the label is trendy. The clothes I go for are the sort that all the people I hang about with wear... it originally came out of skate-boarding and surfing. It's not ordinary high street because it's more expensive and in special shops. It may sound snobby, but I'd say that only intelligent, maybe better class people wear this stuff. It's not "pretty" or fashionable. It's trendy, which is different.

'The boys wear big, baggy trousers and tops and trainers and sometimes baseball caps. The girls have sleeker tops and skimpy little mini-skirts or tight trousers or jeans. Everything has a logo on it that you can see and sometimes more than two other labels on the outside. People who aren't into this look, which is druggy, I admit, don't understand what it is and it makes us into a special social group. You have to have money (or your parents do) to buy this stuff. I think these clothes will develop more in the next few years and the 'social' thing of identifying with labels will continue.

'The labels I think will always be big are: Mambo – designed for surfers, so mainly beachwear. Very baggy for the boys, tiny dresses and very tight tops for girls. Very good clothes and bags and everything. Trigger Happy – mainly for girls. Hussey – for girls. There's also a label called "Slapper". Lots of these have cut-outs and zips in them. Hooch – bright colours; mainly for boys but does a girls' range called Fehm. Quicksilver – surfy clothes for boys, usually in dull colours. Alien Workshop – mainly for boys, T-shirts, etc. Very baggy but clever logos that I like a lot. Technics – horrible baggy tops for boys with big logo. Minute shirts for girls.

'With lots of this stuff, the name could be that of a big company that's behind car technology or space-travel or something but they let their name be part of boys' wear because it sounds macho. The girls' wear is meant to be just decorative, I suppose.'

Until she reached the sixth form, Lady Jane has daily worn school uniform, of course.

A LOVELY HIP-LENGTH, slightly fitted shirt, tunic or short mini-dress (I'm not certain which) made from soft, 'distressed' denim. It has a silver stud button-through and is very well made. Label: 'Perfect Mixed. The intellectual know that Nature is the basis of our knowledge. World Wide Quality 100% pure cotton'. About 1990.

MY FIVE-YEAR-OLD GRANDSON suggested I put his new satchel in the book. It's a black PVC material (13 × 14 inches), bound with grey tape with plastic safety clips and shoulder harness. On the flap is a padded mask of Star Wars baddie Darth Vader. Label: 'Special Star Wars Trilogy Edition.

THE ARBITER REPLIES

In reply, the Arbiter of Good Taste, who is two years older than Lady Jane and goes to a local comprehensive school (they are firm friends and often swap clothes) says:

'Jane is a fashion manufacturer's victim. I think the clothes she and her friends wear are clone-ish and boring because they are so groupy. You might as well wear a uniform. I actually think it's common to dress in such an obvious way. It shows lack of confidence. I believe clothes should express your individuality – having taken in certain fashion details, if you like them. Samantha [eldest sister] has huge style and you can't buy that. She wears her clothes wonderfully. That makes her stand out, not what she wears. I remember when she was a student she bought everything from charity shops and she looked brilliant; she made her own look. It's like they say, 'fashion fades but style remains': you can't fake it or get it by wearing logos and labels. If you have no imagination or originality you have a boring look. Clothes are very important to me, not because they're 'cult' or 'trendy' but because they are part of my creativity and reflect my inner feelings and personality. I think I will always love feminine, mysterious, timeless clothes like Ghost, and I admit I like very good jeans and trousers to go with simple, unfussy tops that I buy anywhere because I like them, not because of the label.

'When I've finished my exams, I'm going to start making my own clothes. Please, will you and Daddy buy me a sewing-machine for my birthday?'

This is a good insight into the compelling hold the fashion industry has over the young – and the not so young. To represent the plethora of young labels, I have chosen an 'Oasis' badge that is a super-star from the 1990s and belongs to the Arbiter.

Made in China'. Charlie also suggests that any Batman clothing will be worth collecting when he's big. May I add that I think that Teletubbies are going to be all the bubble, so look out for T-shirts illustrating the characters.

P AIR OF WHITE AND SILVER fabric 'fashion' plimsolls or daps. Did you know Samuel Plimsoll, one time coal merchant and then MP for Derby, was known as 'the Sailors' Friend'? He campaigned vigorously for the Merchant Shipping Act of 1876 and the Plimsoll-line limit of loading is named after him – as are the canvas deck shoes. 'Dap' is an old word meaning to bounce or dip. 1995.

Bought by the vicar
for the Arbiter (on
her instructions) for
her Sixth Form dance,
Christmas 1996.

ANKLE-LENGTH, BLACK AND white lace sausage-skin dress with high, 'Hong Kong' neckline, made from Lycra and something, fully lined. Label: 'Wallis'. **£70/$115** new and it's a classic. (*See Plate 13.*)

A LARGE 'BUGATTI' (CURVED TOP) make-up or sponge bag made from tortoiseshell-patterned vinyl with a zipper. Stamped on heavy gilt pull: 'Acca Pacca' (and oak leaf motif). The last word in elegance and you wouldn't mind being caught rushing to the bathroom with it. **£39/$65** new.

DULL GOLD, METAL-FACETED collar in an Ancient Greek style with large dolphin and pearl pendant. Stamped 'Askew'. 1996. Sue Askew is the designer who made this limited edition piece. It's very light and comfortable to wear. 1996. **£65/$108.**

PAIR OF CHUNKY GOLD metal and amethyst paste drop earrings, marked 'Fior', in original box. Fior were established London jewellers from 1892 who, very wisely, turned to paste during the 1920s when there was a huge demand for costume jewellery. They specialize in fine quality work that looks like the real thing and have supplied small wants to such knowing customers as Joan Collins and Elizabeth Taylor. About 1990. **£6.50/$11.**

JEWELLERY

Pretty Victorian silver jewellery is still sought and lockets are desirable. You can have jokey and articulated contemporary pieces made from a variety of materials, even re-cycled 'junk'. I am fascinated by the temptingly beautiful work done in papier mâché, synthetics and non-precious metals. Some lovely pieces were made from old drinks cans. I never buy expensive trinkets for the collection. If I am paying lots of money for a piece of jewellery then it is going to be something that I will wear and use within the collection if needed.

The vicar would say
crosses have never been
out of fashion in nearly
2000 years, but I feel
this upsurge of interest
was more to do with
the other Madonna.

A WHITE, HEAVY BRAID choker with small gold cross pendant. Crosses, little and large, were in for the first half of the 1990s. **50p/80 cents.** The look goes with this Jean-Paul Gaultier corseted scent bottle from 1994.

A PAIR OF IMITATION, oak-leafed, tortoiseshell sunglasses. Classic 'Grace Kelly' shape. They have a dinky, duster yellow carrying pouch and come in a splendid cylindrical box in blue and white. Frightfully expensive at £89/$146, but totally chic and collectable.

THE DEATH OF THE PRINCESS

The days that followed the death of the Princess of Wales on 31 August 1997 were full of grief and disbelief. I and many others wore black ribbons (and the vicar wore a purple one made from ribbon commemorating her marriage), but as a fashion historian I looked at the crowds to see whether there were other forms of mourning dress being worn. A friend witnessed three young girls outside Kensington Palace, crying together, arms linked, all wearing white T-shirts with 'WHY WHY WHY?' printed on the front and 'Only the Good Die Young' on the back. One day, such poignant, spontaneuous sartorial responses to this tragedy will be treasures.

MEN'S UNDERWEAR 1990

I T IS FITTING THAT A BOOK about clothes should end in France. In a century of underpanting, these French knickers of the 1990s break new ground. I present 'Ho1' by Hom. Short white trunks (hang on, it gets more exciting) with swing label saying multi-lingual things like '... new extraordinary fibre mixture of cotton (67%) and modal (25%) with elastance (8%) is extremely stretchy ... guarantees maximum comfort ... excellent wearer properties. The material has a pleasantly soft handle ... luxurious silky appearance ... specially easy care. Ecologically tested ... to OEKO-TEX Standard 100...'. OK, but what has this Hom got that pants of the past hundred years haven't had? **Le braguette horizontale**. He really is Lord of the Flies.

USEFUL THINGS TO KNOW

A WORD OF WARNING

Before you start collecting clothes, I beg you to think about where you're going to put them. 'Oh, I've got a bit of room in...' won't do, because if the collecting bug takes over you will be bursting at the seams in no time. Although we have a fairly large (decaying) parsonage that once housed children as well as costume, it now only has room for the Arbiter of Good Taste (a late arrival) because as the children left, the costume seemed to take over. If it overflows downstairs, the vicar gets very cross and we 'have words', as my granny used to say. Be warned that you either need more space than you think or an accommodating partner.

PRACTICAL NEEDS FOR COLLECTING COSTUME

Storage space: cool, dark (keep curtains drawn)

Acid-free tissue paper (lots)

Trunks, skips (big wicker baskets), suitcases

Clean boxes, large and small (long florists' boxes are excellent)

Plastic storage trays

Padded hangers - make your own

Old sheets for dust covers, wraps and for lining trunks and boxes

Strong dress rails

Tie-on labels for clothes

Stick-on labels for boxes

A book to record all the details about the items you acquire... unless you can do it on computer

Moth-balls and other moth-repelling agents

Needlework tools, including a tape measure and safety-pins (I have found the best way to transport clothes is in 'bodies': pile dresses flat on a sheet, wrap the ends and secure with safety-pins.)

Clothes' brushes

Magnifying glass (unless you have superb eyesight, you need this to examine stitching, etc.)

A dress-makers' dummy or two

Handling costume

Museum costume and textiles people always handle artefacts
wearing white cotton gloves (because the natural grease on
our skin adheres to cloth). I don't do this with my collection,
but I always wash my hands before I touch the clothes.
Be sensible and careful about who you allow to handle the
costumes. Some people are monstrously insensitive or have
hot sweaty hands (shove gloves on them!).

Suppliers

Acid-free tissue paper can be supplied in bulk by Conserva-
tion Resources, Unit 1, Pony Road, Horspath Industrial Estate,
Cowley, Oxford OX4 2RD. Tel: 01865 747755; fax: 011865
747035. A bill roll (37 inches × 109 yards) will cost about
£46. Smaller quantities can be bought in sheets from Arts
and Crafts shops.

Dress-makers' dummies. You can make your own (see Janet
Arnold's book in *Further Reading*); you may happen to find an
old one in an antique shop; or you can use a modern 'Venus'
or wire one covered with wadding. But if you wish to acquire
a new period-looking dummy, get a catalogue from Siegel
and Stockman, 2 Old Street, London ECIVV 9AA. Tel: 0171
251 6943; fax: 0171 1250 1798. They have a huge selection
in different styles.

Cleaning old clothes

Use your intelligence. If you know it will wash and not 'run'
or shrink, then wash it. If it is strong enough to dry clean,
take it to any high street cleaners. If a treasure, older, or
covered in sequins, embroidery, etc., take it to a specialist
cleaner and let them look at it. If stained, dirty, antique and
valuable, seek the advice of a museum conservator. If you
are still in doubt, leave it as it is. A dirty garment is better
than a totally ruined one.

FURTHER READING AND USEFUL PEOPLE AND PLACES

There are thousands of books about costume history, as you will see if you flick through local library lists, but the following have been constantly rewarding and informative.

ARNOLD, JANET, *A Handbook of Costume*, Macmillan, London, 1973. A splendid, useful book full of information about conserving clothes, making dummies, museums that house clothes, etc. Janet Arnold is an acclaimed costume historian.

BACLAWSKI, KAREN, *The Guide to Historic Costume*, Batsford, London, 1995. Tells you about actual clothes stored in museums in the U.K.

BRADFIELD, NANCY, *Costume in Detail: 1730 to 1930*, Harrap, London, 1969. My favourite book on costume, a veritable bible. Bradfield's beautiful, exacting drawings of garments – inside and out – make this a peerless book.

CLANCY, DEIRDRE, *Costume Since 1945*, Herbert Press, London, 1996. Excellent fashion drawings with amusing, well-researched commentary on *couture*, street and anti-fashion.

CUNNINGTON, P. AND MANSFIELD, ALAN, *Handbook of English Costume in the 20th Century (1900-1950)*, Faber & Faber, London, 1973.

CUNNINGTON, P. AND WILLETT, C., *Handbook of English Costume in the 19th Century*, Faber & Faber, London, 1959.

CUNNINGTON, P AND WILLETT, C., *The History of Underclothes*, Faber & Faber, London, 1951.

Dr and Mrs Cunnington (and Mr Mansfield) wrote oodles about male and female costume, all detailed with lots of references. The Cunningtons founded The Gallery of English Costume at Platt Hall, Manchester.

O'Hara, Georgina, *The Encyclopaedia of Fashion: 1840s to 1960s*, Thames and Hudson, London, 1986. Useful when searching for a fashion date, a designer's name or the reason why such and such got called that, etc.

Ruby, Jennifer, *Costume in Context*, Batsford, London, 1980 ff. Title of a series of books on various aspects of costume. Clear, bright drawings and text based on real people – wonderful for children, students or collectors. The series goes from the early centuries to the present day.

Sometimes it is difficult to obtain out-of-print books other than through a library or an antiquarian bookseller who specializes in costume and textiles, such as:

John Ives, 5 Normanhurst Drive, Twickenham, Middlesex TWI INA. Tel: 0181-892 6265; fax: 0181-744 3944.

Ann Morgan-Hughes, Meadow Cottage, High Road, Wortwell, Harleston, Norfolk IP20 0EN. Tel: 01986 788826.

Felicity J. Warnes, 82 Merryhills Drive, Enfield, Middlesex EN2 7PD. Tel: 0181-367 1661; fax: 0181-372 1035.

All the big museums that display costume usually have relevant books for sale.

Museums

Every city or large town has a local history museum that has some items of costume on display. If you wish to look at something in the reserve collection, you would be advised to write to the curator and make an arrangement to view. There are collections of costume at several National Trust properties throughout the country.

DIRECTORY OF COSTUME DEALERS

The following are dealers from whom I have purchased items for my collection:

Maggie Adams and Ken Jones, Collectable Costume,
Fountain Antique Centre, Bath.
Tel: 01225 428731.
19th / 20th-century clothes, accessories and jewellery.

Meg Andrews,
23 Cowper Road, Harpenden, Hertfordshire AL5 5NF.
Tel: 01582 460107; fax 01582 461112.
18th / 19th / 20th-century clothes, shawls, purses. Expert on oriental textiles.

Mary Cooper,
The Guinnel, Harrogate, North Yorkshire.
Tel: 01423 567182.
19th / 20th-century clothes and accessories – specializes in fans.

Echoes,
650A Halifax Road, Eastwood, Todmorden, West Yorkshire.
Tel: 01706 81777505.
Bags, purses, shoes, hats, clothes, linens from 19th / 20th centuries.

Joan Griffiths, 'Nostalgia',
Wednesday Market Antiques, Tetbury, Gloucestershire.
Tel: 01666 505039.
1920s onwards. Clothes and accessories. Specializing in mid-20th-century costume jewellery.

Ruth Hand, Hand in Hand, 3 North West Circus Place, Edinburgh EH3 6ST.
Tel: 0131 226 3598 (fax the same).
19th / 20th-century clothes, accessories, jewellery, shawls, etc.

LONDON DEALERS

Alfie's Antiques Market,
13-25 Church Street, Marylebone, NW8.
There are several stalls which sell period costume and accessories from the 20th century.

American Classics Vintage,
404 King's Road, SW10.
Tel: 0171-351 5229.
Original clothes from the 1940s to the 1970s. Levis and WWII flying jackets.

Annie's Antique Clothes,
10 Camden Passage, Islington, N1.
Tel: 0171-359 0796.
19th / 20th-century clothes.

The Antique Clothing Shop,
282 Portobello Road, W10.
Tel: 0181-964 4830.
Clothes from 1860 to 1960.

The Gallery of Antique Costume and Textiles,
2 Church Street, Marylebone, NW8 8ED.
Tel: 0171-723 9981.
Lavish 18th / 19th / 20th-century frocks and textiles – from expensive to 'Wow!'

Blackout II,
51 Endell Street, Covent Garden, WC2.
Tel: 0171-240 5006.
Old and very old kitsch; glitz and glamour and much else from the 1920s to the present day.

Modern Age and Vintage Clothing,
65 Chalk Farm Road, NW1.
Tel: 0171-482 3787.
Collectors' clothes from the 1930s to the 1970s.

Steinberg and Tolkien,
193 King's Road, SW3.
Tel: 0171-376 3660.
Expensive, bizarre clothes and accessories from 1840 to 1980.

Virginia,
98 Portland Road, Holland Park, WII.
Tel: 0171-727 9908.
Exquisite, decorative clothes and underwear
from the 1920s and 1930s.

'295',
295 Portobello Road, W10. No phone.
Everything from the 1960s or earlier if
relevant to fashion now.

OTHER BRITISH SOURCES

There are costume and accessories dealers
throughout the UK, and if you are keen you
will soon seek out your own stockists. A full
and helpful list is found in *The Antiques Shops of
Great Britain*, published annually by the
Antique Collectors' Club. *The London Fashion
Guide* by Mimi Spencer, published by Evening
Standard Books, 1997, lists second-hand and
vintage shops in London.

Cheap Date is a magazine that specializes in
'thrift' and does a witty tramp of charity
shops and other economic emporiums on
your behalf. £1 bi-monthly, P.O. Box 16778,
London ECIM 5XA.

All auction houses have clothes and accessories for sale from time to time, and the
larger houses (Christie's, Sotheby's, Phillips
and Bonhams) have specialist sales every few
weeks. Write or phone for catalogues.

The Costume Society, founded in 1965, has
worldwide membership and is devoted to
costume, fashion and textile history in every
form. The journal *Costume* is published annually and contains many scholarly articles on
all aspects of dress. The Society arranges lec-
tures, seminars and museum visits at home
and abroad. The Membership Secretary is Ms.
Pat Poppy, M.A., A.L.A., 56 Wareham Road,
Lychett Matravers, Poole, Dorset BH16 6DS.

NEW YORK DEALERS

The Enchanted Room,
65-67 Sheather Street, Hammondsport,
New York, 14840.
Tel: 800 544 0198.
20th-century clothes.

Family Jewels,
823 6th Avenue, New York.
Tel: 212 679 5023.
20th-century designer clothes.

Cora Ginsburg,
815 Madison Avenue, New York, NY 10021.
Tel: 212 744 1342.
A famous dealer in 18th/20th-century clothes,
lace and quilts. Well patronized by museums.

Harriet Love,
412 West Broadway, New York, NY 10022.
Tel: 212 737 7671.
20th-century clothes in good condition.

OTHER AMERICAN SOURCES

To make a comprehensive list of dealers
throughout the U.S. would require another
book! Suffice it to say that they flourish from
Arizona to Wisconsin. In American 'Yellow
Pages' dealers may be listed under 'Antique
Clothes' and also under other headings,
such as 'Resale', 'Vintage' or 'Second-hand
Clothing'.

It is possible to subscribe to the Costume and
Textile Auctions at Christie's South Kensington
through Christie's East, New York.

The Costume Society of America is at 330
West 42nd Street, Suite 1702, New York,
NY 10036. It publishes the journal *Dress*
annually.

Acknowledgements

My grateful thanks to:

Cynthia Noble, house clearer extraordinaire, who for years has found me treasures, sumptuous, simple and surprising.

Jean Beresford for the most amazing potato-sackfuls ever.

Kathleen Meredith for fascinating trifles.

Valerie Threlfall, Jeni Wise, Gill Twigg, Jean White, Margaret Ulyatt, Christine Taylor, Jill Poppleton, Irene Taylor and Hilary Dean-Hughes for miles of conversation, loads of help and tons of friendship.

Cynthia Atherton Brown, for a heritage beyond price.

Nancy Cobb, for clothes and their dates.

Mary Ireland for initial costume history lessons.

Nancy Bradfield for inspiration.

My local charity shops (Break, Sue Ryder and Tenovus) and all those who have generously given me clothes and accessories for the collection. I owe you everything.

My publishers and all the members of the team who helped to produce this book.

My family, who for years have had to put up with domestic inconvenience due to me and my costumes... and to Ollie, for loving me in spite of them.